English Grammar and Vocabulary Practice Exercises for all

Felicien Dago

By the same author

Politics, Economics and Development
in Sub-Saharan Africa

The IMF, the World Bank, Humanitarian
Organisations and Development

THE DATE

Write in letters. Write in full.

Example:
15 January: <u>January fifteenth</u> or <u>the fifteenth of January</u>
4 March: <u>March fourth</u> or <u>the fourth of March</u>

1) 1 April   _____

2) 2 May   _____

3) 3 June   _____

4) 4 July   _____

5) 21 August   _____

6) 22 September   _____

7) 23 October   _____

8) 24 November   _____

9) 31 December   _____

10) 5 January   _____

11) 8 February   _____

12) 9 March   _____

DEMONSTRATIVE PRONOUNS

Look at the picture and complete the sentence with the correct word: *this, that, these,* or *those.*

	SINGULAR	
Near		_____ orange is for me.
Far		I am saving _____ orange for my brother.

	PLURAL	
Near		_____ oranges are for the party.
Far		I will take _____ oranges to my grandparents.

AM, IS, ARE

Choose the right word to complete the sentence.

1) Mr. Townsend _____ our new teacher.
2) We _____ in the best class.
3) How _____ the weather there?
4) I _____ not at the library.
5) Where _____ you?
6) Jason and Ahmed _____ not in the basketball team.
7) _____ I late?
8) Sally _____ not the team captain.
9) _____ they from Portugal?
10) Roger and I _____ taking the bus.
11) _____ my brother and I invited?
12) The police _____ investigating the incident.
13) Your cousins and I _____ learning Spanish.
14) Where _____ the keys?
15) Rashed and his friends _____ not here yet.

WILL, WILL NOT

Choose the right word(s) to complete the sentence.

1) Sameh _____ pay you back today. He has no money now.
2) _____ the match start at 18:00?
3) No, I _____ call you today. I am too busy.
4) Who _____ take David's place on the team?
5) Ali and Peter are running late. I am afraid they _____ be able to get here on time.
6) When _____ he finish the report?
7) Where _____ you be in twenty years?

WAS, WERE, WAS NOT, WERE NOT, DID, DID NOT

Choose the right word(s) to complete the sentence.

1) Today is Tuesday. Yesterday _____ Sunday.
   Yesterday _____ Monday.
2) Mariam and Nourah are sisters.
- _____ they go to the same primary school?
- Yes. But, they _____ not in the same class. So, they _____ not have the same teacher.
3)
- How _____ your holiday in Spain? _____ you have a good time?
- No. The weather _____ not great: it _____ raining all the time!

HAS, HAVE

Choose the right word to complete the sentence.

1) Ahmed _____ a new job.
2) I _____ an appointment at the bank.
3) Mrs. Nolan _____ opened another coffee shop in Liverpool.
4) Does Sandra _____ a brother?
5) Femi _____ no time today.
6) The new students _____ just received their books.
7) We still _____ time. We don't _____ to rush!
8) Middle Eastern countries _____ a lot of oil.
9) The police _____ arrested the suspects.
10) Do you _____ an extra notebook?
11) They don't _____ the answer to these questions.
12) _____ the driver called you yet?

PREPOSITIONS: IN, ON, AT with time expressions

Choose the right word to complete the sentence.

1) Rachelle will be in England _____ May.
2) Omar always wakes up _____ 6:30.
3) The conference started _____ 10 o'clock _____ the dot.
4) The lift is being repaired. _____ the meantime, please use the stairs.
5) Will you be doing something special _____ your birthday?
6) Kate was born _____ April 22, 1998.
7) _____ the news, the children got upset.
8) Did you travel to Dubai _____ 2020?
9) School starts _____ Monday.
10) Lunch is _____ noon.
11) Shall we meet _____ Wednesday morning?
12) Raoul found his passport and was able to join us _____ the last minute.
13) The shops don't open _____ night.
14) The Principal will call you _____ the end of the day.
15) They always go to Switzerland _____ winter.
16) The managers are having a meeting _____ the moment.
17) The mailman will bring the parcel _____ half an hour.
18) _____ one point, she went in the kitchen to take a phone call.
19) You will see us _____ dinner.
20) Please be ready: we leave _____ sunrise.
21) There will be a parade _____ Independence Day.
22) Did their parents go to Mauritius _____ their anniversary?
23) We used to do it that way _____ the past.
24) Let's have that drink _____ the evening.
25) Can we come and see you _____ any time during the day?

26) It's important to be punctual and to be _____ time.

* Prepositions are not needed for time expressions like: last week, yesterday, next week, soon, today, earlier, now, later, tomorrow, recently...

Examples:
Can you call me *tomorrow*?
The meeting is taking place *next week*.
The football match will start *soon*.

DID, DID NOT, DOES, DOES NOT

Choose the right word(s) to complete the sentence.

1) Yuki went to Denver. She _____ go to Atlanta.
2) _____ your computer work? I need to print my homework now!
3) Brian _____ find the keys he lost yesterday.
4) _____ she know how to drive? We can't wait. We need to go now.
5) Pierre _____ know how to cook. He is always eating out.
6) If the rain _____ stop, we won't be able to go out this afternoon.
7) _____ you forget your book in the library?
8) _____ Miriam study with you in college ten years ago?
9) How much _____ this dictionary cost these days?

PAST SIMPLE

REGULAR (-ed) and
IRREGULAR (non -ed) verbs.

Complete the sentence with the PAST SIMPLE tense/form of the verb in brackets.

1) The students (to start) the course in September.
2) Samantha (to give) me a folder for you.
3) We (to be) on holiday. We (to go) to Mexico.
4) He (to paint) his room green.
5) The Dean (to greet) all the teachers.
6) The General (to observe) the situation very carefully, and (to tell) the soldiers to get ready.
7) My cousin Maria (to buy) a car and (to teach) me how to drive.
8) The driver (to wash) the cars yesterday.

9) Michael and his friends (to play) video game all night. They also (to make) a lot of noise.
10) I (to finish) early and (to bring) you flowers.
11) Her husband (to bake) her a cake for her birthday.
12) It (to rain) for days. That (to make) the roads slippery; so I (to brake) carefully in order to stop the car.

COMPLETE THE TABLE WITH THE CORRESPONDING VERB OR ADJECTIVE.

VERBS	ADJECTIVES
To differ	
	Confident
To depend	
	Obedient
To present	
To insist	
	Excellent
To converge	
	Recurrent
To absorb	
	Deterrent
	Repellent
To suffice	
	Convergent
To diverge	
To inherit	
	Constituent

ADJECTIVES ENDING IN −ED and −ING.

Choose the right word to complete the sentence.

1) This book is *amazed/amazing*! I like the story.
2) The student was happily *surprised/surprising* by the gift.
3) The players are *tired/tiring* after training all day.
4) Turn if off! What a *bored/boring* movie!
5) This part of the competition can be very *challenged/challenging*.
6) The child is *confused/confusing* by the bright lights from the cameras.
7) Skydiving is very *excited/exciting*!
8) Thunder and lightning can be *frightened/frightening*.
9) The performance of his team has been *disappointed/disappointing*.
10) This kid can be very *annoyed/annoying*: he won't shut up!
11) She is taking a cat to the Vet for a minor operation. She is a little *worried/worrying* right now.
12) The class found the show *interested/interesting*!
13) Stop! I am serious. I don't find it *amused/amusing*.
14) You will be *shocked/shocking*. We couldn't believe it either!
15) It is *surprised/surprising* that the authorities still haven't said anything. The people are starting to get *frustrated/frustrating*.
16) The children are *bored/boring* with seating there quietly: let's do something fun.
17) The customer was *infuriated/ infuriating* by the shop's response to her questions.
18) The dog was only *interested/interesting* in the food.
19) When Samira saw the snake, she was *terrified/terrifying*. It's such a *terrified/terrifying* animal!

20) The tourists were really *fascinated/fascinating* by the ancient buildings.
21) Stop it! You can be so *exhausted/exhausting*!
22) Linda thinks her husband is *charmed/charming*: he always has something nice to say.
23) The students had a long holiday. They all seem very *relaxed/relaxing*.

COMPLETE THE TABLE WITH THE CORRESPONDING VERB OR ADJECTIVE.

VERBS	-ED ADJECTIVES	-ING ADJECTIVES
please		
		challenging
	exhausted	
embarrass		
	interested	
relax		
	overwhelmed	
captivate		
	annoyed	
		astounding
inspire		
	charmed	
	moved	
worry		
		convincing
depress		
	frustrated	
surprise		
	fascinated	
	relieved	
		shocking
confuse		
satisfy		
	bored	
	thrilled	
		exciting
	tempted	
alarm		
terrify		
	tired	
soothe		
	amused	

		liberating
		amazing

TO TEACH, TO LEARN
TO LEND, TO BORROW

Complete the sentence with the correct form of the right verb.

1) My aunt will _____ me how to drive this afternoon. She is a great teacher: I am sure I will _____ a lot.
2) Can you _____ me $20. I will give it back when we get home.
3) The player was _____ to Real Madrid for a season.
4) They need to _____ your dictionary. Don't worry; they will bring it back as soon as they finish.
5) I was _____ by the greatest trainer in the whole wide world: my big brother!
6)
- The bank _____ us all the money for the business ten years ago.
- How much did you _____ from the bank?
7) Nourah _____ herself how to play the piano for months now.

ME, MYSELF, I and OTHERS.

Complete the table with the correct corresponding words.

Subject Pronouns	Object Pronouns	Possessive Adjectives	Possessive Pronouns	Reflexive Pronouns
	me		mine	
you (singular)				yourself
he		his		
	her			
it				
we	us			ourselves
you (plural)		your		
they		their		

Complete the sentence with the correct word from the table above.

1)
- Rita, this is my book. Where's _____?
- _____ is in my bag.
- Lucky you! Andrew and Brenda are still looking for _____.

2) John and Joanna bought _____ a brand new car.

3) Is Michaela going back to _____ country this holiday?

4)
- Why is Maria late?
- _____ woke up late. And _____ car wouldn't start!
  Her father had to give _____ a lift this morning.

5) The cat saw _____ in the mirror.
   It looks like it likes _____ reflection in the mirror.

6) We moved into _____ new house last weekend.
   This huge garden is all _____!

7) _____ am going to call the driver when I find my phone.

I see you are busy. I will look for _____ all by _____.

8) Peter and Rosa, you will be all by _____ on next week's shift.

Will _____ be all right?

9) Miss Alvarez came to the conference with _____ children. _____ must be very proud of them. _____ were extremely smart.

10)
- What's the matter?
- I am in Miss Browne's class! _____ lessons are boring. _____ never explains things properly.

11) We will be waiting to hear from you.

Just give _____ a call whenever you are ready to proceed.

12) Why isn't he answering _____ phone?

13)
- How do _____ like your meal, Sir?
- _____ is excellent. Thank you very much.

14)
- Aaron and Samantha, did you do your homework _____?
- Yes, we did _____ all by _____.

15) Our neighbours are lovely people.

_____ are nice people to live next to.

_____ children are very well behaved.

SO... and TOO to say "ALSO", "AS WELL"; and the opposite: "EITHER" and "NEITHER".

Example:

POSITIVE	NEGATIVE

Chloe: I am going to Australia.
 	
Alice:
- I am going to Australia **too**.
 	
     Or
 	
- **So** am I.
	Charles: I am *not* going to Australia.
	
	Elisabeth:
	- I am not (going) **either**.
	
	     Or
	
	- **Neither** am I.

John: I play tennis regularly.
 	
Terry and Sacha:
- We play tennis regularly **too**.
 	
     Or
 	
- **So** do we.
	Gemma: I don't play basketball often.
	
	Tess and Sandra:
	- We don't play basketball often **either**.
	
	     Or
	
	- **Neither** do we.

POSITIVE	NEGATIVE

Choose the correct answer.

1) You are not late.
a) So are Miriam and Nourah.
b) Either are Miriam and Nourah.
c) Neither are Miriam and Nourah.
d) Too are Miriam and Nourah.

2) Suki has finished her essay.
a) So did we.
b) So do we.
c) So had we.
d) So has Khaled.

3) The team captain was excellent.
a) So were the game.
b) So were his teammates.
c) So are his teammates.
d) So was his teammates.

4) The post office isn't open.
a) Neither is the bank.
b) Either is the bank.
c) Neither isn't the bank.
d) Either isn't the bank.

5) The electrician came at ten o'clock.
a) So has the plumber.
b) So did the plumber.
c) Either did the plumber.
d) So was the plumber.

6) We don't have time.
a) Either do I.
b) Neither do I.
c) Do I either.
d) I do neither.

7) Rita is excited about her exam score.
a) So we are.
b) We are so
c) So are we.
d) So did we.

8) They haven't made any mistakes.
a) She hasn't either.
b) She has not.
c) She did.
d) Neither haven't you.

9) The meeting wasn't cancelled.
a) Either was the conference.
b) Neither were the conference.
c) Neither was the conference.
d) Neither have the conference.

COMPLETE THE TABLE WITH THE CORRESPONDING VERB OR ADJECTIVE.

VERBS	ADJECTIVES
	Hesitant
	Observant
	Resistant
To tolerate	
	Pleasant
	important
To tolerate	
To assist	
	ignorant
To contest	
To expect	
	Dominant
To defy	
To insist	
	Migrant
To vacate	
	Compliant

PUT THE WORDS IN ALPHABETICAL ORDER.

1. exam 2. eye 3. eraser 4. extraordinary 5. exhausted	

1. attitude 2. attention 3. appropriate 4. asphyxiation 5. accuracy 6. addition	

7. gravity 8. politics 9. numbers 10. situation 11. monopoly 12. rhetoric 13. joke 14. octopus 15. umbrella 16. jacket	

SPORTS, HOBBIES and VERBS: PLAY, DO and GO

Choose the right verb and put it in the correct tense to complete the sentence.

1) We will *do/go/play* tennis this summer.
2) You really should *do/go/play* running more often: it will help you relax.
3) Amy and her friends were *do/go/play* yoga in the park yesterday.
4) The teachers are *do/go/play* fishing in the lake.
5) When she was younger, Rosa used to *do/go/play* judo.
6) To be this good, Mbappe must have *do/go/play* football all his life!

Choose the right verb *do/go/play* for the activity or sport.

_____ sit-ups	_____ badminton
_____ bowling	_____ ice hockey
_____ hiking	_____ ping pong
_____ ice-skating	_____ soccer
_____ swimming	_____ squash
_____ basketball	_____ volleyball
_____ hockey	_____ baseball
_____ push-ups	_____ dancing
_____ aerobics	_____ chess
_____ exercise	_____ games
_____ cycling	_____ cards
_____ a warm-up	_____ golf
_____ roller-skating	_____ jogging
_____ scuba diving	_____ skating
_____ snow boarding	_____ surfing
_____ diving	_____ sailing
_____ camping	_____ tai chi
_____ archery	_____ kayaking
_____ bungee jumping	_____ horse riding

	table tennis		jiujutsu
_____	video games	_____	puzzles
_____	snooker	_____	ballet

NUMBERS

Write the numbers in letters.

Numbers	Letters
121	
148	
157	
298	
1000	
1894	
28988	
383467	
1765884	
98	
40	
55	
4	
5	
8	
6	
5	
15	
50	
500	

SINCE, FOR, AGO

Choose the right word to complete the sentence.

1) _____ Martin got back from the seminar, he's been very focused on his work.
   a) Since
   b) For
   c) Ago

2) We bought this house ten years _____.
   a) since
   b) for
   c) ago

3) The driver has been waiting _____ twenty minutes. He's been here _____ 11 o'clock.
   a) since
   b) for
   c) ago

4) The manager worked there _____ years before retiring.
   a) since
   b) for
   c) ago

5) It hasn't stopped snowing _____ Monday.
   a) since
   b) for
   c) ago

6) Could you keep an eye on my laptop _____ a moment, please?
   a) since
   b) for
   c) ago

7) My friends have lived in China _____ 2012.
a) since
b) for
c) ago

8) Have the guests been waiting _____ long?
a) since
b) for
c) ago

9) They haven't seen each other _____ high school!
a) since
b) for
c) ago

10) Did they come to the island ten months _____?
a) since
b) for
c) ago

COMPLETE THE TABLE WITH THE CORRESPONDING ADJECTIVE OR ADVERB.

ADJECTIVES	ADVERBS
Correct	
	Beautifully
	Naturally
Quiet	
Loud	
Cautious	
	Gently
Confident	
Anxious	
	Cheerfully
Comfortable	
Perfect	
	Swiftly
Prompt	
Nervous	
	Quickly
Rapid	
	Frequently
Easy	
	Angrily
Patient	
	Smoothly
	Finally

IF

Choose the right word(s) to complete the sentence.

1) If Samiah had money, she _____ buy a new phone.
a) will
b) would
c) would have bought

2) If I _____ time, I will call you.
a) has
b) had
c) have

3) If you _____ water to zero degree Centigrade, it turns to ice.
a) frozen
b) freezer
c) freeze

4) Ricardo _____ that job in Russia, if he hadn't been married.
a) would have taken
b) would take
c) took

5) The Security Guard wouldn't have called the police, if it _____ a serious matter.
a) was
b) hadn't been
c) has not

6) The receptionist will call you, if your parcel _____.
a) arrived
b) arrives
c) will arrive

IF

7) Hussein would not miss the train, if he _____ home early.
a) leaves
b) lived
c) left

8) Quentin _____ his brother, if their father hadn't asked him to make an effort.
a) would never have forgiven
b) will not forgive
c) would not forget

9) You _____ gotten wet, if you had taken an umbrella.
a) was
b) will not
c) would not have

10) If they don't _____ early, they might miss the meeting.
a) lived
b) leave
c) left

11) If she focuses on her studies, Anne _____ pass her exams.
a) need
b) should
c) should have

12) Her father would have bought her a car, if she _____ her exam.
a) have passed
b) has passed
c) had passed

13) Water boils if you _____ it to 100 degrees Celsius.
a) heat
b) hot
c) heated

Join the two sentences with *if*.
Example:
Your cousin isn't here. We will leave without him.
If your cousin isn't here, we will leave without him.

14) You take your car. I can buy the petrol.

_____

15) Your motorbike is in the workshop. You can take mine.

_____

16) The trainer had time. He would contact the player.

_____

17) We were retired. We would travel around the world.

_____

18) The players had won enough matches. The team would have avoided relegation.

_____

19) We would not have been stranded in the middle of nowhere. The driver had remembered to take the spare tyre with us.

_____
_____
_____

COMPLETE THE TABLE WITH THE CORRESPONDING ADJECTIVE OR NOUN.

ADJECTIVES	NOUNS
ill	
	Nervousness
Happy	
Ready	
	Politeness
	Friendliness
Dark	
Soft	
	Bitterness
Lazy	
Thick	
	Smoothness
	Emptiness
	Dizziness
Clever	
	Hardness

PRESENT SIMPLE

Choose the right word(s) to complete the sentence.

1) The leaves of the trees _____ in autumn.
a) fill
b) feel
c) fall
d) felt

2) I _____ new to this college.
a) are
b) am
c) is
d) have

3) How old _____ Anita and her twin sister?
a) is
b) has
c) are
d) have

4) Where _____ the Principal go on holiday?
a) has
b) does
c) have
d) do

5) Martha _____ an appointment this afternoon.
a) has
b) does
c) have
d) do

6) Our neighbours _____ speak Italian.
a) do not
b) doesn't
c) hasn't
d) haven't

7) _____ I say your name correctly?
a) Doesn't
b) Do
c) has
d) have

8) Anita wants to be a journalist, so she _____ the newspaper every day.
a) read
b) reads
c) rode
d) road

9) The shed _____ have any space.
a) do
b) does not
c) donut
d) haven't had

10) Miss Ross and her sister _____ like cold tea, but Mr. Ross _____.
a) does, do
b) do not, doesn't
c) don't, does
d) don't, don't

11) Sally and Peter _____ the same age.
a) have
b) take
c) are
d) run

12) Miss Ross _____ coffee, and I _____ too.
a) like, do
b) likes, does
c) likes, do
d) like, does

13) How many children _____ they have?
a) does
b) don't
c) do
d) doesn't

14) You _____ go to the gym every day, and neither _____ I.
a) go, don't
b) goes, do
c) go, does
d) don't, do

15) Michael _____ speak Portuguese. I _____ either.
a) don't, don't
b) doesn't, doesn't
c) do, doesn't
d) doesn't, don't

16) Ahmed always _____ his homework by himself.
a) done
b) has done
c) does
d) do

17) Every time she _____ abroad, my aunt _____ me a gift.
a) go, has brought
b) gone, bring
c) goes, brings
d) has gone, had brought

PAST SIMPLE

Choose the right word(s) to complete the sentence.

1) Amy: Did you _____ the storm last night?
a) ear
b) heard
c) hear
d) here

Sandra: No, I _____. I _____ fast asleep.
a) did, were
b) didn't, was
c) don't, am
d) do, was

2) _____ Hassan finish his work on time yesterday?
a) Does
b) Do
c) Did
d) Don't

3) All the doors and windows _____ left open last weekend!
a) were
b) was
c) did
d) have

4) The neighbours did not _____ the chairs back.
a) brought
b) brink
c) bring
d) bringed

5) Samira _____ good grades in school.
She _____ a powerful lawyer after university.
a) has, becomes
b) had, became
c) have, became
d) to have, to become

6) Where _____ the mechanic park the car?
a) do
b) has
c) did
d) have

7) Why _____ the office call me last night?
a) does
b) do
c) didn't
d) hasn't

8) Their children _____ born in Egypt.
a) was
b) where
c) wear
d) were

9) These students _____ afraid of hard work!
a) have
b) haven't
c) weren't
d) did

10) This table _____ reserved for the players.
a) has not
b) did not
c) was not
d) doesn't

11) _____ you ready to play?
a) Did
b) Do
c) Were
d) Have

12) Sorry. Ryan and George _____ find their jerseys.
a) didn't
b) haven't
c) hadn't
d) doesn't

COMPLETE THE TABLE WITH THE OPPOSITE CORRESPONDING ADJECTIVE, AS PER THE EXAMPLE.

illegal	legal
Unfriendly	
	Kind
Unconscious	
	Tidy
Unimportant	
Unauthorised	
	Possible
	Clear
illiterate	
irrelevant	
	Responsible
imperfect	
Undemanding	
Dishonest	
incapable	
Disorganised	
inadequate	

A and AN

Choose the correct answer: *a or an* to complete each expression.

1) The international committee will be chaired by _____ African, _____ American, _____ Asian, _____ Australian and _____ European.
2) All officials must wear _____ uniform.
3) What _____ enriching experience!
4) You attended _____ university, didn't you?

Choose the correct answer: *a or an* to complete each expression.

... nice car	... expensive book	... town
... watch	... long interview	... amazing city
... small table	... actress	... large apartment
... red umbrella	... American movie	... easy game
... important dictionary	... Italian actor	... excellent idea
... image	... delicious meal	... valuable opinion

Choose the right word to complete the sentence.

1) You must make _____ appointment to see the doctor.
a) a
b) an
c) and
d) ant

2) Their aunt needs _____ electrician for their house wiring.
a) a
b) an
c) and
d) ant

3) Raise your hand if you have _____ question.
a) a
b) an
c) and
d) ant

4) When are they going to give you _____ definitive answer?
a) a
b) an
c) and
d) ant

5) I just need _____ answer sooner rather than later!
a) a
b) an
c) and
d) ant

6) Taking _____ expensive loan from the bank won't be of any help.
a) a
b) an
c) and
d) ant

7) The class will have _____ exam in a few weeks.
a) a
b) an
c) and
d) ant

8) Aren't we supposed to take _____ final exam?
a) a
b) an
c) and
d) ant

9)   The instructor used _____ perfect illustration.
a)   a
b)   an
c)   and
d)   ant

10) We are looking for _____ illustrated dictionary.
a)   a
b)   an
c)   and
d)   ant

11) It's _____ well-preserved ancient temple.
a)   a
b)   an
c)   and
d)   ant

COMPLETE THE TABLE WITH THE CORRESPONDING VERB OR NOUN.

VERBS	NOUNS
To retire	
	Government
To measure	
	Appointment
To employ	
	Enlistment
To disagree	
	Agreement
To argue	
To judge	
	Requirement
To attach	
	Placement
	Treatment
	Advertisement
To entertain	
To postpone	

NUMBER, NOUN, NOUN

Choose the correct answer to complete the sentence.

1) Alissa bought a house. It has four bedrooms.
   It's a _____ house.
   a) for-bedroom
   b) four-bedrooms
   c) four-bathroom
   d) four-bedroom

2) We spent three hours at the concert.
   It was a _____ concert.
   a) free concert
   b) three-hour
   c) three-hours
   d) three-owl

3) I spent forty pounds on the ticket.
   It was a _____ ticket.
   a) forty-pound
   b) fourty-pound
   c) four-pounds
   d) front pond

4) The hotel is rated as four stars.
   It's a _____ hotel.
   a) for-star
   b) for stars
   c) four star
   d) four-star

5) They will be gone for six days.
This is a _____ trip.
a) six days
b) six day
c) six-day
d) six-days

6) That was a drastic change: the firm used to organise _____ events!
a) nine-days
b) nine day
c) nine-day
d) nine days

7)
- What's going on? Are we moving from _____ to something different?
a) three-steps processes
b) three-step process
c) three step processes
d) three-step processes

- Yes. The directors decided to upgrade our courses. _____ _____ _____ too cumbersome, redundant and costly.
a) Five-steps, procedure, is
b) Five-step, procedures, were
c) Five-step, procedures, is
d) Five step, procedure, were

ADJECTIVES and ADVERBS

Choose the correct answer to complete the sentence.

1) My driving instructor is an experienced trainer.
   He drives very *careful/carefully*.
2) This exercise is *easy/easily*.
3) *Careful/Carefully* drivers never drive
   reckless/recklessly.
4) The soldiers fought *brave/bravely*.
5) They woke up *late/lately*.
   They are going to be *late/lately* to work.
6) Some questions are *hard/hardly*.
   Just keep working *hard/hardly*.

JUST and SOON

Choose the correct answer to complete the sentence.

1) We'll have dinner *just/soon*.
2) The football match *just/soon* ended.
3) The students have *just/soon* finished their exams.
   They'll get the results *just/soon*.
4) *Soon/Just*, Ali's family is going to move to Rome.
5) The school *just/soon* bought new computers.
6) The teacher has *just/soon* spoken with your parents.
   They will be here very *just/soon*.
7) The rain will *just/soon* stop.

VERBS and NOUNS

Complete the table with the corresponding verb or noun.

VERBS	NOUNS
To train	
	Education
	Meeting
To participate	
To collaborate	
	Damage
	Cooperation
	Display
To sign	
To invite	
	introduction
	Success
To celebrate	
	instruction
To locate	
To collect	
To operate	

VERBS	NOUNS
To reduce	
To retire	
	Conquest
To multiply	
	Addition
	Rejection
	implementation
To respond	
	Union
To evaluate	
	Assessment
To conclude	

	Correction
	Negotiation
To produce	
	Confirmation
	Assumption
	Cooperation
To confuse	
To select	
To promote	

AFTER and BEFORE

Choose the correct answer to complete the sentence.

1) Monday comes *after/before* Tuesday.
2) Dessert is *after/before* the meal.
3) I'll get home late. Call me after/before I go to bed.
4) Sally will have a party *after/before* her graduation.
5) The maid just cleaned the floor.
   Take your shoes off *after/before* you enter the house.
6) The principal wants to see you *after/before* you have completed your project and *after/before* you head to Dubai.

SOMETHING, NOTHING and ANYTHING

Choose the correct answer to complete the sentence.

1) Do not say *nothing/anything* you will regret!
2) They had *nothing/anything* to do.
3) We have *anything/nothing* to discuss!
4) The cat was looking for *nothing/something* to eat.
5) The driver had *nothing/anything* to say.
6) *Something/Anything* happened to him. That's why he's upset. He still won't talk about it.
7) A lioness will do *nothing/anything* she can to protect her cubs.
8) The trainer has *something/anything* to do with the success of the team!
9) Maria: Are you doing *nothing/something* at the moment?
   Tracy: No, I am not doing *nothing/anything*.

VEHICLES

	IN, ON	OUT, OFF
car	in	out
taxi	in	out
truck	in	out
bus	on	off
ship	on	off
plane	on	off
boat	in	out
bike	on	off
helicopter	in	out

Examples:
- As soon as you *get in* the car, fasten your seatbelt.
- After the plane landed, I *got off* after collecting my backpack from the overhead cabin.
- At the petrol station, the driver *got out* **of** the truck and bought some fruit and water.

COMPARATIVE and SUPERLATIVE ADJECTIVES

Choose the correct answer to complete the sentence.

1) Is Messi *faster/fastest* than Ronaldo?
2) London is one of the *more/most* expensive cities in the world.
3) After joining the gym, he feels *fitter/fittest* than before.
4) I think Spanish is *easier/easiest* than Korean.
5) Maybe water is the *healthier/healthiest* drink ever.
6) When his country lost the final of the World Cup must have been the *sadder/saddest* day in his life.

ADJECTIVES and VERBS

Complete the table with the corresponding adjective or verb.

ADJECTIVES	VERBS
deep	
weak	
	blacken
	thicken
	sweeten
loose	
dark	
tight	
	harden
sharp	
	redden
	sicken
	fatten
wide	
	awaken
strength	
white	
sad	
	shorten
flat	
broad	
length	
	heighten
	lighten
bright	
deaf	
	fatten
	deafen
mad	
	stiffen
coarse	

COMPARATIVE and SUPERLATIVE ADVERBS

Choose the correct answer to complete the sentence.

1) The winner sang the best/better of all the contestants.
2) The brown horse runs faster/the fastest than the dark one.
3) My team arrived the earliest/earlier than today.
4) You spoke more confidently/the most confidently than your friend.

ADJECTIVES and VERBS

Choose the correct answer to complete the sentence.

1) The parents were awake/awakened by the cries of the child.
2) The unexpected news made them very sad/saddened.
3) The shirt's sleeves are too long. You will have to short/shorten them.
4) The team was bold/emboldened by their three previous victories.

TO PAY with or without Prepositions

Choose the correct answer to complete the sentence.

1) How did you pay _____ the meal?
a) in
b) for
c) by
d) with

2) I paid _____ cash.
a) on
b) for
c) by
d) within

3) Donna had to pay _____ _____ the delivery.
a) the driver, with
b) on, by
c) the driver, for
d) in, the deliveryman

4) This bill must be paid _____ the 4th of the month!
a) in
b) by
c) with
d) up

5) Last month's rent will be paid _____ this month's.
a) from
b) to
c) alongside
d) by

6) The manager told me I could pay _____ my card.
a) on
b) for
c) at
d) with

7) The customers paid _____ and left the restaurant.
a) fantastic
b) for
c) the bill
d) to

8) Sheila has finally paid _____ her credit card debts!
a) of
b) off
c) at
d) to

9) According to the judge, the balance had to be paid _____ thirty days.
a) with
b) within
c) at
d) on

10) You can pay _____ pounds sterling or _____ euros.
a) on, in
b) into, to
c) in, in
d) alongside, with

EVER and NEVER

Choose the correct answer to complete the sentence.

1) Have you _____ been to Dubai?
a) ever
b) never

2) Yes, I have been to Dubai many times. But, I have _____ been to Abu Dhabi.
a) ever
b) never

3) How is Abu Dhabi? I haven't _____ visited that city.
a) ever
b) never

4) It's a nice city. A word of advice: don't _____ go there in summer. It's too hot! Winter is the best season for such a trip.
a) ever
b) never

5) Thank you. It is noted: I will _____ _____ travel to the region during hot seasons.
a) ever
b) never

6) Don't _____ do that!
a) ever
b) never

COMPLETE THE TABLE WITH THE CORRESPONDING VERB OR NOUN.

VERBS	NOUNS
To expect	
	invitation
To solve	
To apply	
	Satisfaction
	Destruction
To describe	
To recommend	
To organise	
To prepare	
	Memorisation
To prioritise	
	intention
	Observation
	Cancellation
To complete	
To repeat	

NEGATIVE SENTENCES

Choose the correct answer to complete the sentence.

- **Past simple**
1) They *did not finished/didn't finish* their work.
2) Rita *did not do/didn't did* her bed this morning.
3) I *didn't want/did not won't* to wake you up.
4) Ahmed *didn't fell/did not fall* in the bathroom.

- **Present simple**
1) The teacher *doesn't drives/does not drive* to college.
2) I *am not/isn't* ready to travel overseas.
3) The cat *is not/aren't* under the bed.
4) Do *not call/doesn't call* me before 10:00!

- **Future simple**
1) The rain *will not stops/won't stop* anytime soon!
2) The classes *won't starts/won't start* till next week.
3) I *will not calls/won't call* you today.
4) We *will not been/won't be* home before 21:00.

- **Past progressive or continuous**
1) You *weren't/was not* running fast.
2) She *hasn't doing/was not doing* the ironing.
3) The child *wasn't/were not* sleeping in his bed.
4) The cars *were not/wasn't* being cleaned properly.

- **Present progressive or continuous**
1) I *am not/aren't* speaking to you.
2) You *aren't/is not* doing yourselves any favours!
3) This horse isn't *feeling/isn't fallen* well.
4) We *are not going/is not going* on holiday this summer.

- **Present perfect**
1) We haven't *finished/finish* yet.
2) She *hasn't started/haven't started* her driving lessons.
3) The rain *have not stopped/hasn't stopped* yet.
4) I *have never being/have never been* to Seattle.

QUESTIONS

Choose the correct answer to complete the sentence.

- **Past simple**
1) Did you bring/brought your books?
2) When did you *see/seen* the keys for the last time?
3) How did they *do/done* this homework?
4) Didn't he *forget/forgets/forgot* to lock the door?

- **Present simple**
1) *Has/Is* the Principal in his office?
2) Why *are/am* you late?
3) Hello! *Ant/Aren't* you supposed to be in a meeting?
4) *Haven't/Isn't* Peter on our team?

- **Future simple**
1) When will the mechanic *fix/fixed* the car?
2) Where will you *be/been* at lunchtime?
3) Why won't they *buy/bought* the bigger house?
4) Who will *look/looked/looking* after the children?

- **Past progressive or continuous**
1) Mary, *was/were* you trying to call me?
2) Were our parents *lived/living* in Ireland in the 1990s?
3) *Was/Has/Have* Peter finishing his dissertation when you saw him?
4) Was/Weren't/Have the students doing their homework in the library?

- **Present progressive or continuous**
1) *Am/Are* I doing the right thing?
2) *Are/is* the guests being looked after properly?
3) Why *aren't/isn't/hasn't* John and Suzie driving their children to school?
4) Who *are/have/had* you speaking to?

- **Present perfect**
1) Why *hasn't / haven't* you called the Police?
2) Where *have / has* the driver taken the car?
3) Have the candidates *arrived / arriving* yet?
4) Who *haven't / hasn't* the new coach already met?

COULD, CAN, MUST, SHOULD, OUGHT TO, MAY, MIGHT, WOULD, WILL

Choose the correct answer to complete the sentence.

1) Hello! Welcome to Best Hotel. *May / Will* I help you?
2) You've been coughing for months. You *should / would* stop smoking.
3) This is not a request: you *might / must* be at work on time all the time!
4) *Can / Ought to* tell me where the Post Office is, Please?
5) If I were you, I *would / can* choose the big house.
6) *Could / Should* you get me a glass of water?
7) How *should / ought to* you operate this machine?
8) The committee *will / ought* get together again tomorrow morning.
9) How *will / ought to* the players get home?
10) It is cloudy: *it might / must* rain.

COMPLETE THE TABLE WITH THE CORRESPONDING VERB OR NOUN.

VERBS	NOUNS
	invasion
	Erosion
	confusion
To suppress	
To conclude	
To intrude	
	Discussion
	Expression
	Diversion
To compress	
To decide	
	Explosion
	Exclusion
To obsess	
	Collusion
To collide	
	Adhesion

CHOOSE THE CORRECT WORD FROM THE BOX BELOW TO FILL THE GAP IN EACH SENTENCE, IN THE TEXT.

> internet, the, in, time, ago, weather, than,
> even, such, renowned, from, to

Fifteen years _____, I travelled _____ Australia. It is about two whole days by plane _____ London.

Australia is famous for many things, _____ as the kangaroos and _____ boomerang.
The _____ in Australia usually very nice.

I spent some _____ in Sydney and _____ Melbourne.
I _____ traveled to New Zealand: home to the world- _____ All Black Rugby team.

Travelling is great. It is better _____ just learning about the world from books or from the _____.

For each gap, CHOOSE THE CORRECT WORD from the corresponding list of words to complete each sentence, in the text.

Smartphones are great (1) _____. They allow us to read, write, work, play, learn and do a great (2) _____ of other things.

Thanks (3) _____ these new technologies, we can be (4) _____ Tokyo and talk to someone in Toronto as (5) _____ they were in the same city. (6) _____ a result, it is often said that the world is (7) _____!

But as French philosopher Rabelais, famously (8) _____ said, "Science without conscience is only ruin of the soul".

This technology (9) _____ to used and interacted with (10) _____.

Not everyone online is motivated by honourable (11) _____ good intentions.

(12) _____, one should always be cautious what they access and interact with on the internet; in order to keep on benefiting (13) _____ its abundant and numerous resources.

1-   a) tool b) talents c) tools d) stools
2-   a) letters b) number c) box d) pack
3-   a) by b) too c) to d) from
4-   a) inn b) in c) and d) to
5-   a) it b) its c) ill d) if
6-   a) At b) It c) As d) For
7-   a) sinking b) standing c) running d) shrinking
8-   a) one b) on c) once d) while
9-   a) as b) has c) have d) had
10-   a) care b) caring c) carefully d) carelessly
11-   a) an b) about c) and d) end
12-   a) There b) Because c) Then d) Therefore
13-   a) for b) from c) on d) at

COMPLETE THE TABLE WITH THE CORRESPONDING NOUN, ADJECTIVE OR VERB.

NOUNS	ADJECTIVES	VERBS
Simplicity		
		Terrify
	Ample	
		Falsify
		Classify
	Certain	
Rectification		
	Specified	
Pacification		
		Glorify
	Qualified	
Unification		
	Fortified	
		identify
	Ratified	
Clarification		
Mystification		
	Notified	
Purification		
	intensified	
	Justified	
		Certify
		Modify

ADJECTIVE and PREPOSITION

Choose the correct answer to complete the sentence.

1) The inspectors were interested _____ the company's procedures.
a) on
b) at
c) in
d) of

2) The students were tired _____ watching TV.
a) for
b) in
c) to
d) of

3) All the employees must be familiar _____ the procedures.
a) on
b) with
c) from
d) by

4) Everyone on the team is responsible _____ health and safety.
a) by
b) upon
c) for
d) at

5) That was kind _____ François to come to your birthday party.
a) on
b) of
c) to
d) in

6) Alicia eventually got tired _____ her doll.
a) up
b) down
c) of
d) in

7) The students are keen _____ inviting a celebrity for the graduation.
a) in
b) at
c) on
d) with

8) The bus was full _____ loud supporters.
a) of
b) on
c) for
d) at

9) This food is different _____ what you usually have at home.
a) at
b) for
c) from
d) about

10) Would your cousins be interested _____ the latest movies?
a) at
b) on
c) in
d) from

11) No one was angry _____ you!
a) with
b) to
c) from
d) by

12) There's no need to be afraid _____ the dark.
a) in
b) at
c) of
d) to

13) The children were upset _____ the lost toys.
a) in
b) on
c) with
d) about

14) The soldiers have been involved _____ the rescue operation.
a) to
b) in
c) from
d) at

15) The tourists got accustomed _____ the weather after a few days.
a) on
b) for
c) to
d) onto

16) We were all exhausted _____ climbing for hours.
a) from
b) in
c) at
d) up

17) Anita is angry _____ the other driver for causing the crash.
a) from
b) about
c) at
d) to

18) The new security guard is incapable _____ handling the queues by himself.
a) with
b) of
c) about
d) onto

19) The employees are opposed _____ the change of hours.
a) on
b) onto
c) to
d) with

20) The salesperson is good _____ sealing deals.
a) on
b) at
c) to
d) from

21) This moment is appropriate _____ further training.
a) from
b) for
c) in
d) at

22) Your phone is similar _____ Joan's.
a) by
b) on
c) from
d) to

23) The phone call was related _____ the conference.
a) into
b) onto
c) from
d) to

24) The company has been successful _____ securing the contract.
a) on
b) by
c) in
d) from

25) The children are keen _____ colourful pictures and drawing.
a) in
b) on
c) with
d) for

26) He never gets tired _____ driving, does he?
a) of
b) by
c) for
d) at

27) The players got tired _____ waiting.
a) to
b) of
c) in
d) at

28) The class is excited _____ the trip to the science museum.
a) on
b) about
c) in
d) to

29) These programs are different _____ the last ones.
a) for
b) from
c) into
d) by

COMPLETE THE TABLE WITH THE CORRESPONDING NOUN, ADJECTIVE OR VERB.

NOUNS	ADJECTIVES	VERBS
Public		
	Categorised	
Modernity		
Normality		
		Minimise
	Criminal	
Advice		
		Televise
Supervision		
	Advertised	
		Disguise
Surprise		

TEACH and LEARN

Choose the correct answer to complete the sentence.

1)
 - Where did you *learn/teach* to speak English so well?
 - My brother *learned/taught* me.
2) You can *learn/teach* almost anything if you are prepared to work hard.
3) That student is a fast learner. He *learns/teaches* everything so fast!
4) The new instructor could *learn/teach* the students so well that they all passed the exam!
5) I wish to *teach/learn* ice-skating. Can you *teach/learn* me?

BORROW and LEND

Choose the correct answer to complete the sentence.

1) Can you *borrow/lend* me some money, please? I will pay you back as soon as we get home.
2) Can't you *borrow/lend* some money from your brother? I left my wallet in the car.
3) Where is the book that the library *borrowed/lent* you?
4) The library didn't *borrow/lend* me any book!
5) Are you sure? Didn't you *borrow/lend* the book for your essay from the library?
6) Roger had to *borrow/lend* his sister's car this morning. His one wouldn't start this morning.
7) Who *borrowed/lent* the neighbours a lawnmower?
8) Why couldn't your friends *borrow/lend* Tony a dictionary for the homework?

MORE VERBS!

Choose the correct answer to complete the sentence.

1) How could you *tell/told* my secret to the whole class?
2) What? I never *tell/told* your secret to anyone!
3) I *feel/fall* so betrayed...
4) I *felt/fell* it was important to you. So, how could I *tell/told* anyone else? Especially when you specifically *sold/said/sell* it was a secret! My parents *caught/taught* me better than that.
5) You can save it. I am not *felling/falling* for that. Whether my car is a second-hand one, it is nobody's business. I *thought/bought* it with my very own money.
6) Wait a minute! If your secret *get/got* out, that *had/have* nothing to do with me.

COMPLETE THE TABLE WITH THE CORRESPONDING VERB/NOUN OR ADJECTIVE.

VERBS/NOUNS	ADJECTIVES
To afford	
To accept	
reason	
respect	
	Reliable
	Believable
	Sensible
	Permissible
	Edible
To refund	
To enjoy	
To understand	
	Moveable
	Repairable
To negotiate	
To debate	
To love	
	Eligible
To neglect	
	Suggestible
	Adorable

AND or BUT

Choose the correct answer to complete the sentence.

1) They want to go on holiday *and/but* they don't have any money.
2) We didn't know each other *and/but* we got on well and/but talked for hours!
3) Kenny misses his family *and/but* he needs to call home this weekend.
4) I am tired *and/but* I am going to bed.
5) Put the water in the cup *and/but* add sugar *and/but* milk.
6) The rain is falling *and/but* the wind is blowing.
7) Kimberly needs some new shoes now *and/but* she has to wait for her wages.
8) Mousab's fridge is empty *and/but* he's going grocery shopping in minutes.
9) We will have to learn how to cook *and/but* clean, all by ourselves.
10) Her parents are in town *and/but* they won't have any time to visit us.

PHRASAL VERBS: some examples

Choose the correct answer to complete the sentence.

1)   The secretary will set _____ the meeting for April 18th.
a)   in
b)   on
c)   up
d)   by

2)   The plane took _____ half an hour ago.
a)   at
b)   off
c)   up
d)   by

3)   If you don't agree with this decision, you can take this matter _____ with the manager.
a)   on
b)   to
c)   up
d)   by

4)   Alex and Alice don't want to be in a relationship anymore. They are going to _____ up.
a)   fight
b)   run
c)   break
d)   listen

5)   After checking the numbers on her ticket, Helena _____ out that she had won the lottery.
a)   thought
b)   run
c)   found
d)   jumped

6) Do not give _____! Stay focused. You will eventually get much better grades.
a) on
b) into
c) up
d) at

7) Burglars _____ into the house next door last night. They took the TV, jewelry and some expensive paintings.
a) run
b) broken
c) broke
d) stole

8) Everyone _____ up! The lesson has now been moved to Room 15.
a) look
b) hear
c) listen
d) check

9) Your brother is at the airport to _____ you up.
a) speak
b) drive
c) pick
d) pack

10) Can you please speak _____? I can't hear you.
a) more
b) loud
c) at
d) up

11) Sometimes, it's wiser to just shut _____ and listen.
a) out
b) to
c) up
d) on

12) In many countries, people _____ off their shoes before entering the house.
a) remove
b) wash
c) take
d) taken

13) _____ on driving: we are almost there.
a) Curry
b) Carry
c) Focusing
d) Slow

14) The price of oil just _____ up!
a) go
b) run
c) want
d) went

15) All parents want to bring _____ their children to be great human beings.
a) in
b) by
c) up
d) up to

16) His whole family was counting _____ him. He couldn't let them _____.
a) for, down
b) down, on
c) on, down
d) to, by

17)
- What does "Constitution" mean?
- Look it _____ in your dictionary.
a) out
b) on
c) up
d) in

18) Enrique's car has _____ down three times already this week.
a) driven
b) break
c) broken
d) stopped

19) Please don't stop! Carry _____ _____ your work.
a) with, on
b) out, with
c) on, with
d) up, at

20) Matthew respects his brother a lot; and looks _____ to him.
a) out
b) on
c) like
d) up

21) I don't believe the price of food is _____ down any time soon.
a) running
b) decreasing
c) coming
d) breaking

22) Whenever Mary goes on holiday, her mother looks _____ her pets.
a) in
b) after
c) for
d) over

23) Don't leave the empty water bottles and coffee cups on the table: throw them _____ in the rubbish bin.
a) in
b) a way
c) away
d) while

24) Please, _____ off the meeting till everyone gets here.
a) plan
b) lead
c) hold
d) delay

25) The managers finally agreed _____ the workers.
a) to
b) by
c) at
d) with

26) The mother sings a soothing song to help the baby _____ down.
a) sleep
b) relax
c) calm
d) smooth

27) Who wakes you _____ in the morning?
a) in
b) up
c) by
d) for

28) The government will apologise to the parents _____ the burst pipe that destroyed the local school.
a) for
b) on
c) because
d) at

29) This can't be true, can it? Admit you are making it all _____!
a) to
b) by
c) up
d) in

30) Liz found her keys: they _____ up under the sofa.
a) woke
b) stayed
c) turned
d) went

31) I only answer _____ the President!
a) on
b) by
c) onto
d) to

32) You need to abide _____ the laws of the country.
a) on
b) by
c) onto
d) to

SINGULAR – PLURAL nouns

Write the missing singular or plural of the noun.

singular	plural	singular	plural
receipt		dress	
	books		buses
plane		class	
	ideas		glasses
boy			inches
	tables	box	
choice		address	
	chairs		watches

singular	plural	singular	plural
family			children
city			men
party			teeth
body			feet
university			knives
melody			shelves
lady			women
monopoly			mice
army			loaves
lobby			leaves

MORE NOUNS

Choose the correct word to complete the expression.

1) a can of _____
a) milk
b) soup
c) soap
d) shampoo

2) a cup of _____
a) coffee
b) candy
c) paper
d) pie

3) a piece of _____
a) milk
b) juice
c) paper
d) sugar

4) a bottle of _____
a) corn
b) beef
c) wine
d) bread

5) a slice of _____
a) bread
b) milk
c) tea
d) chocolate

6) a bowl of _____
a) beef
b) juice
c) fruit
d) shampoo

7) a bar of _____
a) soap
b) soup
c) hot chocolate
d) juice

8) a glass of _____
a) water
b) candy
c) cheese
d) corn

9) a bag of _____
a) soap
b) water
c) chips
d) juice

10) a bunch of _____
a) bananas
b) bread
c) pickles
d) cake

11) a set of _____
a) peas
b) wine
c) screwdrivers
d) gloves

12) a loaf of _____
a) shoes
b) soap
c) fruit
d) bread

13) a pack of _____
a) juice
b) cigarettes
c) chips
d) tea

14) a pair of _____
a) socks
b) bread
c) coffee
d) soup

15) a slice of _____
a) coffee
b) cheese
c) soap
d) chips

16) a sip of _____
a) orange juice
b) salt
c) cheese
d) bread

17) a grain of _____
a) wheat
b) wine
c) chips
d) chocolate

18) a bar of _____
a) chocolate
b) wine
c) bread
d) tea

COMPLETE THE TABLE WITH THE CORRESPONDING VERB OR NOUN.

VERB	NOUN
Exist	
	Dependence
	Difference
insist	
	Presence
	Offence
Silence	
Present	
	Experience
Disobey	
Reside	
	Obedience
Emerge	
Refer	
Adhere	
Cohere	
	Reverence
	Recurrence
Occur	
Coincide	

ACTIVE VOICE and PASSIVE VOICE

Turn the active sentence into a passive one; and the passive sentence into an active one.

Active voice	Passive voice
Peter is driving the car.	
	These cakes were baked by my aunt.
Anita booked the flights.	
	The wall is being painted by a famous artist.
The gardener will take care of the flowers.	
DHL has delivered your documents.	
Mrs. Andrew taught the students well.	

The runner has just broken the world record.	
	They had been detained by Immigration at the borders for hours.
Managers must address those issues.	
They should have dealt with urgent tasks first.	
Our competitor could have won that important contract.	
The company may replace the employees' bus.	
	Some of the key processes will be outsourced by the directors.
The director can postpone the meeting.	

SCRAMBLED WORDS

Here are the names of some *household appliances*.
Could you spell the words correctly?

ekoorc   _____

eigretrrrfoa   _____

veno   _____

ooehvr   _____

erihhswasd   _____

fdgeir   _____

frrzeee   _____

icemaovwr   _____

edlrbne   _____

atroset   _____

mierx   _____

etlkte   _____

rino   _____

eoiievlnts   _____

COMPLETE THE TABLE WITH THE CORRESPONDING NOUN OR ADJECTIVE.

NOUNS	ADJECTIVES
Advantage	
Courage	
Outrage	
	Nauseous
	Gaseous
Right	
	Prosperous
Caution	
Disaster	
Envy	
Danger	
	Anxious
Courtesy	
	Poisonous
Fame	
	Venomous
	Mountainous
	Humorous
Thunder	
Population	
	Mysterious
Tumult	
	Murderous
	Magnanimity
Hazard	
	Luminous
Ruin	
	Gracious
Malice	
Omen	
	Spontaneous
	Calamitous

	Notorious
Ambiguity	
	Adventurous
	Anonymous
	instantaneous
	Tempestuous
Autonomy	
	Simultaneous
	Tenacious
	Glorious

SCRAMBLED WORDS

Here are some nouns related to the *classroom*.
Could you spell the words correctly?
The first letter of each noun is provided.

1. obsko b _ _ _ _
2. sked d _ _ _
3. shirca c _ _ _ _ _
4. uortmecp c _ _ _ _ _ _ _
5. deykabro k _ _ _ _ _ _ _
6. yinaocirdt d _ _ _ _ _ _ _ _ _
7. elspicn p _ _ _ _ _ _
8. psen p _ _ _
9. nhrepraes s _ _ _ _ _ _ _ _
10. eersra e _ _ _ _ _
11. colck c _ _ _ _
12. weomrkoh h _ _ _ _ _ _ _
13. zuiq q _ _ _
14. maex e _ _ _
15. rasged g _ _ _ _ _
16. tsuentsd s _ _ _ _ _ _ _
17. eitetbmla t _ _ _ _ _ _ _ _
18. ecrheat t _ _ _ _ _ _

HOW MANY; HOW MUCH

Choose the correct expression to complete the sentence.

1) How *much/many* months are there in a year?
2) How *much/many* does this book cost?
3) How *much/many* eggs do we need for the cake?
4) How *much/many* milk is there in the bottle?
5) How *much/many* money are your employees being paid?
6) How *much/many* people are coming to the party?
7) How *much/many* do I owe you?
8) How *much/many* water does the captain drink a day?
9) How *much/many* other cities were affected?
10) How *much/many* are you on this bus?
11) How *much/many* time do we have left?

A, AN and THE
Choose the correct word to complete the sentence.

1) I just bought you *a/an/the* book. It talks about healthy eating.
2) What is *a/an/the* capital of New Zealand?
3) Write down *a/an/the* exact meaning of the new words.
4) The speaker made *a/an/the* interesting point.
5) Who is *a/an/the* best football player in *a/an/the* world?
6) When *a/an/the* night falls, many animals go hunting for their food.
7) Only *a/an/the* authorised staff member can sign that document.
8) We are having an interview with *a/an/the* American Ambassador to the UN.
9) *A/An/The* apple a day is good for your health.
10) All *a/an/the* new students need to report to the hall.
11) Why are *a/an/the* dogs barking?

12) IBM is looking for *a/an/the* qualified accountant.
13) In this city, you need *a/an/the* umbrella!
14) *A/An/The* most important thing is to remain excellent.
15) Name *a/an/the* port city in South Korea.

REPORTED SPEECH

Turn the direct speech sentences into reported speech ones.

Direct speech	Reported speech
"I am late for class", Mary said.	
"We won't go on holiday this summer", my neighbours told me.	
"The cat can't climb out of the well by itself", the child complained.	
"We have to knock the buildings down", the authorities declared.	
"I am going to call you", the lawyer told his client.	
"We drove the whole morning", the team leader revealed.	
"Time will always be more important than money", the wise man told his students.	
"It isn't the right tool", the mechanic told his trainee.	
"I have read that book twice", the librarian said.	

SOMEONE, SOMEWHERE ELSE...

Some	one	+	else
Any	body		
No	where		
Every	thing		

Choose the correct word to complete the sentence.

1) Have you spoken to _____ else about this?
a) somewhere
b) everything
c) anyone

2) We really need to park the car _____ else.
a) somewhere
b) everything
c) anyone

3) The migrants have _____ else to go.
a) anyone
b) nowhere
c) something

4) The instruction clearly states: "Leave _____ else and turn up at once!"
a) something
b) everything
c) nothing

5) Sorry. I just can't leave it for _____ else to deal with.
a) somebody
b) nobody
c) anywhere

6) Would you like _____ else to drink?
a) somewhere
b) something
c) nothing

7) Is there _____ else we can do to help?
a) anything
b) someone
c) somewhere

CHOOSE THE CORRECT WORD TO COMPLETE THE SENTENCE.

1) The *beauty/beautiful* of the gardens left visitors speechless.
2) The staff was extremely *help/helpful*.
3) She is so wise that she only says *meaning/meaningful* things.
4) They handled the equipment with *care/careless*.
5) The operation was *pain/painless*. There was no need for anesthesia.
6) The *success/successful* of the new products was due to the team's dedication.
7) Be *care/careful* with the minister's new car. It cost him a fortune.
8) This manual is a great way to improve your English language *skills/skillful*.
9) Playing your music this loud can be *harm/harmful* to your ears!
10) There's a *peace/peaceful* protest taking place downtown.

CHOOSE THE CORRECT WORD TO COMPLETE THE SENTENCE.

1) I'm waiting at the airport where it says *arrives/arrivals*.
2) Their refuse/refusal to honour the contract created the delays.
3) Who is authorised to *approve/approval* this transaction?
4) The landlord is seeking the police's *approve/approval* in order to evict the tenants.
5) Someone needs to *remove/removal* the van from the driveway.
6) Did the hosts put a car at your *dispose/disposal*?
7) Thank you for your *propose/proposal*. The managers will look into it very carefully. They will *peruse/perusal* it at this morning's meeting.
8) Have you ever heard of *survive/survival* of the fittest?
9) The bank is the only place where you can *withdraw/withdrawal* some money.

SCRAMBLED WORDS

Here are the names of some *vegetables*.
Could you spell the words correctly?
The first letter of each noun is provided.

1. cmbucreu	c _ _ _ _ _ _	14. ueacfwllrio	c _ _ _ _ _ _ _ _ _
2. lagric	g _ _ _ _ _	15. rlecye	c _ _ _ _ _
3. ealggnpt	e _ _ _ _ _ _ _	16. negirg	g _ _ _ _ _
4. rdhias	r _ _ _ _ _	17. eivlos	o _ _ _ _ _
5. agbcbae	c _ _ _ _ _ _	18. aapgssaur	a _ _ _ _ _ _ _ _
6. toatop	p _ _ _ _ _	19. upinmpk	p _ _ _ _ _ _
7. otmaot	t _ _ _ _ _	20. ptuinr	t _ _ _ _ _
8. snhcpai	s _ _ _ _ _ _	21. nooin	o _ _ _ _
9. hclii	c _ _ _ _	22. rrcaot	c _ _ _ _ _
10. ormmsuho	m _ _ _ _ _ _ _	23. avdaoco	a _ _ _ _ _ _
11. rcno	c _ _ _	24. ltetuce	l _ _ _ _ _ _
12. peeppr	p _ _ _ _ _	25. acroedinr	c _ _ _ _ _ _ _ _
13. bcoiorcl	b _ _ _ _ _ _ _	26. spea	p _ _ _

94

SCRAMBLED WORDS

Here are the names of different kinds of fruits.
Could you spell the words correctly?

1. lnetmrwoae _ _ _ _ _ _ _ _ _ _

2. anaabn _ _ _ _ _ _

3. picator _ _ _ _ _ _ _

4. npeiapepl _ _ _ _ _ _ _ _ _

5. geiutrfapr _ _ _ _ _ _ _ _ _ _

6. nmgoa _ _ _ _ _

7. umpl _ _ _ _

8. syrerprba _ _ _ _ _ _ _ _ _

9. asepgr _ _ _ _ _ _

10. blybeeurr _ _ _ _ _ _ _ _ _

11. agenartmpeo _ _ _ _ _ _ _ _ _ _ _

12. hrrcye _ _ _ _ _ _

13. teyarrbrsw _ _ _ _ _ _ _ _ _ _

14. eapr _ _ _ _

15. notccou _ _ _ _ _ _ _

16. ahecp _ _ _ _ _

17. kiiw _ _ _ _

18. ifautsripons _ _ _ _ _ _ _ _ _ _ _ _

PREPOSITIONS and VARIOUS USUAL ENGLISH EXPRESSIONS

Choose the correct word to complete the sentence.

1) The Principal told all the students to be _____ their best behavior.
a) at
b) in
c) on
d) for

2) Well, you can't take everything _____ face value.
a) at
b) in
c) on
d) for

3) They all need to figure _____ what their next move is going to be.
a) up
b) on
c) out
d) by

4) "You are all doing great", the coach told the players _____ way of encouragement.
a) for
b) by
c) in
d) from

5) Barbara's father made sure his family lacks _____ nothing.
a) with
b) for
c) from
d) in

6) _____ the direction of the new Managing Director, the company offices were moved to a more affordable building.
a) At
b) Onto
c) In
d) By

7) The stores are having amazing deals _____ low prices.
a) on
b) at
c) by
d) from

8) They will have to come _____ terms _____ the real facts!
a) in, on
b) to, with
c) with, to
d) by, up

9) The farmers gave us some fruit and vegetables _____ exchange _____ books and pens.
a) in, from
b) in, for
c) for, in
d) to, with

10) Keep going. Just keep _____ it! Don't give _____!
a)   at, up
b)   by, up
c)   to, from
d)   for, at

11) Maria is the same age _____ Tony.
a)   to
b)   for
c)   as
d)   from

12) Do you really have any idea what you are getting involved _____; and what you are signing _____ _____?
a)   in, on, at
b)   up, with, to
c)   in, up, for
d)   in, from, by

13) Each argument needs to be considered _____ its own merits.
a)   to
b)   in
c)   with
d)   on

14) The city is cut _____ _____ the rest _____ the country.
a)   with, to, of
b)   of, for, at
c)   off, from, of
d)   in, by, for

15) Christopher arrived _____ his children _____ tow.
a) by, on
b) with, in
c) for, with
d) with, on

16) The teacher told the students to collect all the books they could lay their hands _____.
a) with
b) at
c) on
d) from

17) So, _____ light _____ all the exceptional circumstances we are facing at present, and as your Commander in Chief; I have no other option than to declare martial law.
a) by, on
b) in, of
c) for, to
d) in, for

18) What brings you here _____ this hour?
a) with
b) at
c) to
d) from

19) The table is made _____ wood, metal and glass.
a) off
b) of
c) on
d) by

20) Michael Jordan stands _____ a height of 1,98m.
a)   on
b)   at
c)   in
d)   by

21) Can you strike _____ a conversation with total strangers?
a)   on
b)   with
c)   up
d)   for

22) Taking _____ account to growing population, this community needs bigger schools and hospitals.
a)   from
b)   to
c)   into
d)   with

23) Abigail now works whenever she wants. She is living _____ her investments.
a)   with
b)   off
c)   of
d)   at

24)
   Mike Tyson knocked _____ his opponent _____ seconds.
a)   in, out
b)   out, in
c)   over, out
d)   out, over

They didn't even stand a chance _____ fighting back!
a) on
b) in
c) at
d) up

25) All the leaders decided to agree _____ the Prime Minister, _____ the sake of peace and stability.
a) to, on
b) with, in
c) with, for
d) on, for

26) The driver went home _____ the night.
a) to
b) at
c) for
d) up

27) The cleaners should have it all over and done _____!
a) from
b) with
c) on
d) by

28) Maurice told me I could confide _____ him.
a) with
b) on
c) in
d) at

29) What has become _____ the development project for this region?
a) for
b) of
c) in
d) by

30) Feel free _____ ask any questions you may have.
a) for
b) from
c) with
d) to

31) Joanna's father took an immediate dislike _____ her boyfriend.
a) at
b) on
c) to
d) by

32) The team realised that _____ hindsight they should have played the match in the morning.
a) to
b) in
c) for
d) into

33) I'll be _____ my way.
a) by
b) in
c) on
d) from

34) _____ the looks of things, the economy will recover soon.
a) On
b) By
c) Up
d) At

35) I am simply visiting some friends. I am therefore not here _____ an official capacity.
a) on
b) from
c) in
d) by

36) The authorities are putting a stop _____ all the incompetence!
a) with
b) from
c) in
d) to

37) Amir is a quiet and studious person. He must not have forgotten his book _____ purpose.
a) in
b) with
c) on
d) for

38) Congratulations _____ your graduation: this calls _____ a celebration!
a) in, from
b) on, for
c) by, with
d) within, at

39) They are all going _____ holiday.
a) at
b) in
c) on
d) with

40) Just relax. She will call you _____ her own good time.
a) with
b) in
c) on
d) by

41) There was no doubt _____ what the government was going to do.
a) to
b) at
c) about
d) up

42) Some of the rules must be learned _____ heart.
a) at
b) by
c) in
d) on

43) _____ all it's worth, consider all the options before making _____ your mind.
a) For, up
b) In, on
c) With, up
d) By, to

44) _____ a certain extent, the staff member is right.
a) In
b) For
c) To
d) By

45) You don't want to take our word _____ it; come and see _____ yourself.
a) for, for
b) in, on
c) by, with
d) from, at

46) If you promise to keep it to yourself, she might let you in _____ some of the office secrets!
a) by
b) and
c) from
d) on

47) _____ my humble opinion, this is a great idea!
a) For
b) Onto
c) In
d) By

48) _____ all due respect, that argument is highly questionable.
a) From
b) Up
c) With
d) On

49) They have several properties _____ rent and _____ sale.
a) from, for
b) by, to
c) for, for
d) up, in

50) I am looking forward _____ hearing _____ you again soon.
a) by, for
b) to, for
c) to, from
d) at, on

51) Take it _____ me: the sole purpose of this present manual is to make your English excellent!
a) for
b) with
c) by
d) from

52) Linda retired _____ her job last month.
a) for
b) with
c) by
d) from

53) Let's make a stop _____ the grocery store.
a) to
b) at
c) from
d) in

54) Our neighbours moved: they now live _____ the city's outskirts.
a) to
b) from
c) on
d) onto

55) They found a beautiful house outside _____ London.
a) from
b) of
c) by
d) with

56) Was your nephew offered a job _____ Apple?
a) to
b) at
c) on
d) up

57) Please. Don't rush. We do have plenty _____ time.
a) on
b) off
c) of
d) with

58) For any questions related to corporate vision, please allow me to defer _____ my manager.
a) with
b) from
c) to
d) by

59) I'm afraid: your friends did badly _____ the test.
a) on
b) by
c) to
d) into

60) _____ want of a better term, I will settle _____ "incongruous".
a) For, from
b) For, for
c) By, up
d) On, in

61) Terry achieved all his goals _____ dint of sheer hard work.
a) with
b) by
c) on
d) in

62) The musicians will perform _____ the condition that the concert organisers pay their travel costs.
a) in
b) into
c) for
d) on

63) Ever since she got a well-paying job, the elder sister has been looking _____ _____ all her younger siblings.
a) away, for
b) out, on
c) out, for
d) on, to

64) The managers have been out _____ town for a seminar.
a) in
b) off
c) of
d) by

65) The accountant drew the team's attention _____ the inaccuracies in the reports.
a) with
b) in
c) by
d) to

66) All the people in the neighbourhood were trying to make sense _____ what was happening.
a) off
b) on
c) of
d) in

67) Mr. Khumar's family depended _____ him and his income.
a) at
b) into
c) with
d) on

68) They eventually came _____ the conclusion that moving to another city was the only option.
a) up
b) within
c) in
d) to

69) The investigator became famous for always looking for more information. He barely ever took anything _____ face value.
a) in
b) at
c) for
d) from

70) What important matters did your brothers have to attend _____?
a) in
b) with
c) to
d) from

71) London has great parks _____ abundance.
a) on
b) in
c) from
d) at

72) Smart-Tech used its huge cash reserves _____ its advantage and bought all its profitable competitors. Now, it is the largest Tech firm in the whole world.
a) from
b) with
c) at
d) to

73) The fact _____ the matter is that the government must set up a commission to investigate where all those million pounds of taxpayers' money have gone.
a) with
b) of
c) to
d) up

74) The community has been faced _____ rising unemployment.
a) from
b) with
c) in
d) on

75) The children haven't been doing anything since school ended. They appear to have a lot of time _____ their hands.
a) for
b) on
c) at
d) in

76) The president asked all the officers to meet him _____ once.
a) on
b) in
c) at
d) by

77) The driver was waiting close _____ hand.
a) at
b) in
c) with
d) to

78) They are asking _____ your help.
a) from
b) for
c) in
d) on

79) The children followed _____ quick succession.
a) on
b) in
c) by
d) for

80) _____ first, the objectives were not clear _____ the audience.
a) At, to
b) At, at
c) To, in
d) With, to

81) This car is _____ sale.
a) from
b) for
c) in
d) at

82) What is their plan _____ action?
a) from
b) of
c) by
d) on

83) _____ a number of occasions, the power went _____.
a) In, in
b) On, out
c) At, to
d) From, from

84) _____ obvious reasons, classes have been cancelled.
a) In
b) For
c) At
d) On

85) The encircled fighters eventually came _____ terms _____ their precarious situation and started to surrender.
a) in, with
b) to, with
c) by, in
d) at, on

86) The principal says he will see _____ it that the students _____ your care lack _____ nothing.
a) in, in, from
b) to, in, for
c) on, with, from
d) to, on, for

87) Their presentation still looks like a work _____ progress.
a) by
b) in
c) on
d) from

88) I have the privilege _____ introducing to you your new president.
a) from
b) of
c) off
d) in

89) This message is _____ the utmost importance.
a) on
b) off
c) of
d) in

90) May we remind you that you are accountable _____ the people of this land?
a) in
b) to
c) at
d) from

91) It is so serious that it is punishable _____ expulsion _____ this community!
a) in
b) by
c) to
d) from

92) Breakfast consists _____ plain rice and water.
a)   for
b)   off
c)   from
d)   of

93) In a way, their competitor's failed product launch was _____ the advantage of Smart-Tech company.
a)   with
b)   by
c)   to
d)   within

94) The students often borrow books _____ their friends.
a)   on
b)   of
c)   at
d)   off

95) Because there were so many curves _____ the roads, they had to drive very carefully.
a)   by
b)   for
c)   in
d)   with

96) What was the idea that stuck _____ him the most?
a)   to
b)   with
c)   from
d)   at

97) Each teammate tried his jersey _____ size.
a)   for
b)   on
c)   in
d)   by

98) Ruth was recruited _____ the Secret Service.
a) at
b) by
c) up
d) on

99) Chelsea beat Arsenal _____ a final score _____ 3
    _____ 1.
a) in, at, to
b) with, of, to
c) by, off, at
d) within, onto, after

100) All the officials travel _____ coach.
a) into
b) on
c) by
d) from

101) How long did your cousins plan _____ staying?
a) in
b) on
c) from
d) by

102) They practised so much that they eventually got the
     hang _____ it.
a) on
b) of
c) for
d) off

103) The class did great in the exam. This calls _____ a celebration.
a)   from
b)   in
c)   for
d)   by

104) _____ the click _____ a button, you can book a world tour!
a)   With, in
b)   With, of
c)   By, with
d)   On, to

105) The mechanic had his doubts _____ the car they brought to his workshop. It turns out, it was stolen.
a)   in
b)   on
c)   about
d)   for

106) A famous actress stopped _____ the shop and bought several items _____ clothing.
a)   on, off
b)   by, of
c)   from, in
d)   with, by

107) The voters want to know if candidates have the country's best interests _____ heart.
a)   at
b)   with
c)   from
d)   by

109) Brandon was not _____ fault. The other driver caused the crash.
a) on
b) at
c) with
d) in

110) _____ the risk of trying your patience, listen _____ what your brother is saying.
a) From, from
b) At, onto
c) At, to
d) By, for

111) After the tragic demise of the duke, the whole _____ the kingdom was _____ mourning for a month.
a) of, at
b) of, in
c) in, off
d) at, from

112 Of course, the voters are fully aware _____ the rising prices of food and gas.
a) to
b) off
c) of
d) from
e) on

113) At this university women, men, the rich, the poor... everyone is equal and therefore held _____ the same standards.
a) to
b) off
c) of
d) from
e) on

114) This short manual is only an introduction. It aims _____ giving you a glimpse _____ how exciting and fascinating grammar and vocabulary really are.
a) at, with
b) at, off
c) at, of
d) on, at

115)
- What do you make _____ the new headmaster?
- Dr. Abdullah? He seems kind and very professional.
a) off
b) from
c) of
d) by

116) The HR manager is not _____ liberty to divulge employees' private information.
a) from
b) at
c) with
d) on

117) Were all those matters being properly dealt _____?
a) from
b) at
c) with
d) on

118) In order to win the elections, the campaign team decided to look at their strategies _____ totally different lenses.
a) onto
b) by
c) at
d) through
e) on

119) All the delegates met _____ the president's request.
a) onto
b) by
c) at
d) through

120) The store will replace the faulty part _____ no extra charge _____ you.
a) at, to
b) from, to
c) for, at
d) by, with

121) The secretary hasn't got round _____ the conclusion _____ the report yet.
a) to, at
b) at, to
c) to, of
d) in, from

FILL EACH GAP WITH THE CORRECT WORD TO COMPLETE THE SENTENCES.

Example:
(0) -… winter **and** spring

There are four seasons: summer, autumn or fall, winter (0) _____ spring.
(1) _____ one of these four seasons has (2) _____ own particular characteristics. (3) _____ instance, winter is the 'snow season' whereas autumn - or fall as it's known (4) _____ Northern America - is when trees lose their leaves.

Depending (5) _____ where we live on (6) _____ surface of the earth, we certainly experience each season differently.
And (7) _____ a result, we all probably have (8) _____ favourite season (s).

COMPLETE THE TABLE WITH THE CORRESPONDING VERB OR NOUN.

VERB	NOUN
Assist	
	Guidance
Perform	
	Clearance
Accept	
	ignorance
	Disturbance
insure	
Attend	
	inheritance
Enter	
	Misguidance
	Reassurance
Rely	
Tolerate	
Assure	
	Annoyance
	Remembrance
	Reappearance
Appear	
	Dominance
	Maintenance
	Acceptance
Resist	

PAST PERFECT and PAST SIMPLE

Put each verb in brackets in the appropriate tense.

1) The office (already, to phone) seven times before I even noticed the missed calls.
2) The salesman had already met his target, so he (to be awarded) a bonus.
3) When Idriss entered the class, the lesson (already, to start).
4) We had just made it to the cabin, when it (to start) to rain.
5) The game (to barely start) when the power went out!
6) What had the contractors been doing all the time you (to be) on holiday?
7) Arnold rented out the house that he (just, to buy).
8) Arun (to spend) all his cash before he realised that was his last $50 bill.
9) By the time the president's plane landed, all the officials (already, to be) in place to welcome him.
10) They (never, to hear) of this dish before they (to move) here three years ago.
11) In 2021, Victoria joined Tesla. Prior to that, she (to work) for Microsoft.
12) Had these machines been working properly before the power (to go) out?
13) The audience couldn't believe the magician (to make) a real tree appear on the stage!
14) At first, no one would believe he (actually, to drive off) and (to leave) them standing in the middle of the jungle.
15) The driver (just, to leave) the office when the manager called.
16) Rhonda was thrilled to head to college. She (always, to want) to prepare for her dream job!

17) He (not, to be – *Interrogative and Negative sentence*) in power for decades when he was finally overthrown in a military coup?

18) After she (to pack) her suitcases and (to lock) her doors, Samirah left for the airport.

19) In June, Donald moved to San Diego. Before that, he (to live) in Hungary.

20) The patient (to feel) a lot better after he'd taken his medication.

21) Simon (never, to be) away from home until he started college.

22) The campers thought they (to run out) of food.

23) The neighbours had been tackling the blaze before the fire brigade (to arrive).

24) The students were truly thrilled. That was certainly one of the most fascinating conferences they (ever, to attend)!

25) Dimitri moved to Japan three years ago. He (to work) in Poland twenty years before.

26) The group of students (to insist) they hadn't used those books.

27) The managers (to intend) to have the grand opening, but unfortunately it snowed heavily the entire week.

CHOOSE THE CORRECT WORD TO COMPLETE THE SENTENCE.

1) The lake is _____. It is not artificial.
a) nature
b) natural

2) The _____ limousine is being guarded by General Kroning's men.
a) president
b) presidential

3) You can't ask the teacher's his salary! That's a _____ question.
a) person
b) personal

4) The _____ Minister will be interviewed by the BBC.
a) Finance
b) Financial

5) The police forces are tackling serious _____ activities in that part of town.
a) crime
b) criminal

6) Get out of your city and country. Travel the world. That's certainly the best way to learn about the _____ of other people on earth.
a) culture
b) cultural

7) The _____ who left their bag in the canteen can collect it from Reception.
a) person
b) personal

8) In _____ to the camera, Miriam brought her laptop.
a) addition
b) additional

9) The authorities are planning development projects for this entire _____.
a) region
b) regional

10) Unfortunately, the _____ of the virus is still unknown.
a) origin
b) original

11) A lot of YouTube videos can be used free of charge for _____ purposes.
a) education
b) educational

12) The _____ is dedicated to the treatment of young children.
a) clinic
b) clinical

13) As your _____, I take our _____ security very seriously.
a) President
b) Presidential
c) nation
d) national

14) The company has always been run in a _____ manner.
a) profession
b) professional

15) The Dean has ordered new _____ instruments for the band.
a) music
b) musical

CHOOSE THE CORRECT WORD TO COMPLETE THE SENTENCE.

1) It was an _____ decision to make.
a) easily
b) easy

2) They _____ deflated the tyres to allow the stuck truck to get out of the tunnel.
a) simply
b) simple

3) The new regulations are _____ from today.
a) effectively
b) effective

4) What the managers had to do was _____ just listen to the workers.
a) basically
b) basic

5) Any attacks on our sovereignty and national integrity will be met with _____, very strong retaliatory action!
a) immediately
b) immediate

6) The shipping company delivered the package _____.
a) promptly
b) prompt

7) You should have your tutor explain the answers that were not _____.
a) correctly
b) correct

8) The new director _____ introduced himself to his collaborators.
a) formally
b) formal

9) The rain _____ falls in this part of the world.
a) rarely
b) rare

10) Looking back, that was everything but a _____ idea.
a) sensibly
b) sensible

SOME (adjectives and) ADVERBS OPERATE DIFFERENTLY from those in this exercise.

ADJECTIVES	ADVERBS
good	well
fast	fast
hard	hard
early	early
late	late
far	far
long	long
short	short
straight	straight
fine	fine
daily	daily

Examples:
* The weather is *fine,*
- great
- nice
- lovely...

Fine, great, nice, and *lovely* are all ADJECTIVES.

* The engine works *fine,*
- properly
- correctly
- smoothly
- well
- perfectly
- marvelously...

Fine, properly, correctly, smoothly, well, perfectly and *marvelously* are all ADVERBS.

HAVE, MAKE, GET, LET, AND HELP

Complete the sentence by putting the verb in brackets in the correct tense.

1) Do your parents make you (to do) any chores at home?

2) His brother (to let) him drive his car last week.

3) The new neighbours are having their lawn (to upgrade).

4) Mother (to get) the driver to wash the car again yesterday.

5) The soldiers were helping the rescued tourists (to get) in the helicopter.

6) Let's (to have) the class put some money together for the perfect's birthday cake.

7) When are they going to get the roof (to fix)?

8) Tomorrow, they (to help) us clean the house.

9) Please get the children (to take off) their shoes before coming into the house.

10) Last weekend, you let Ron (to cover) your shift.

11) Come and help us (to move) the couch.

12) Yesterday, the tenants (to make) the owner change the carpet.

13) Amy needs to have her money (to refund).

14) No one can make you (to do) anything you are not willing to do.

15) Have the waiter (to bring) us the menu.

SH or CH

Choose the correct letters to complete the word.

1)	Tea _____ er	113)	_____ enanigan
2)	_____ ark	114)	Mu _____
3)	_____ eep	115)	_____ op
4)	Engli _____	116)	_____ ore
5)	_____ air	117)	_____ are
6)	Fren _____	118)	_____ips
7)	_____ icken	119)	_____ ore
8)	_____ ocolate	120)	Wa _____
9)	Lun _____	121)	Wat _____
10)	_____ ip	122)	_____ ampion
11)	_____ inese	123)	_____oose
12)	_____ oes	124)	_____ ower
13)	Fi _____	125)	Bea _____
14)	_____ ampoo	126)	_____ atter
15)	Kit _____ en	127)	_____ atter
16)	_____ erries	128)	Ben _____
17)	Ca _____	129)	S _____ akles
18)	_____ eck	130)	_____ e
19)	_____ ain	131)	_____ y
20)	_____ op	132)	_____ ampagne
21)	_____ out	133)	Unfurni _____ ed
22)	Tarni _____	134)	_____imney
23)	_____ allenge	135)	Spani _____
24)	_____ ance	136)	Brandi _____
25)	Tra _____	137)	Sun _____ ine
26)	Trea _____erous	138)	_____ ocking
27)	_____ ortage	139)	Ar _____ ery
28)	_____arade	140)	_____ eriff
29)	Ex _____ange	141)	S _____ edule
30)	Wi _____	142)	_____ ariot
31)	Rubbi _____	143)	_____ out
32)	Bru _____	144)	Bran _____
33)	Brun _____	145)	_____ rug

34) Pou _____	**146)** _____ ute
35) Sla _____	**147)** Hit _____
36) Fini _____	**148)** _____ allow
37) Bat _____	**149)** _____ elves
38) _____ ildren	**150)** _____ eetah
39) Di _____	**151)** Pun _____
40) _____ alk	**152)** _____ est
41) Reli _____	**153)** Bun _____
42) Furni _____	**154)** Cu _____ ion
43) _____ art	**155)** Bot _____
44) A _____ amed	**156)** _____ illing
45) _____ un	**157)** Peri _____ able
46) _____ in	**158)** Sa _____
47) _____ rink	**159)** _____ ield
48) Hun _____ back	**160)** Fle _____
49) _____ rimp	**161)** _____ rine
50) _____ arge	**162)** Hen _____ men
51) _____ eet	**163)** Su _____
52) Lee _____	**164)** _____ rub
53) Slo _____	**165)** Fla _____
54) Fre _____	**166)** _____ oulder
55) _____ eat	**167)** _____ allenge
56) _____ oke	**168)** Blea _____
57) Cou _____	**169)** _____ amber
58) _____ ambles	**170)** Member _____ ip
59) _____ ine	**171)** Ri _____
60) Establi _____ ment	**172)** Fla _____ y
61) Pin _____	**173)** Leader _____ ip
62) Mar _____	**174)** _____ oot
63) Ou _____	**175)** Rea _____
64) Mar _____	**176)** Tor _____
65) Tou _____	**177)** _____ epherd
66) Prea _____	**178)** Ar _____ diocese
67) _____ illing	**179)** Ma _____
68) _____ arity	**180)** Flin _____
69) Ar _____	**181)** _____ ivering
70) U _____ er	**182)** Extingui _____ er

71)	Du _____ ess	183)	_____ oo
72)	_____ eque	184)	Nouri _____ ing
73)	Ea _____	185)	Brea _____
74)	_____ arp	186)	_____ ur _____
75)	Flu _____	187)	_____ u _____
76)	_____ ake	188)	_____ urn
77)	_____ impanzee	189)	_____ ief
78)	Sear _____	190)	Spee _____
79)	_____ rivel	191)	_____ uffle
80)	Da _____ ing	192)	La _____ es
81)	Fa _____ ion	193)	Accompli _____ ed
82)	Blu _____	194)	A _____ ievement
83)	_____ ided	195)	Feveri _____
84)	Lavi _____	196)	Whi _____
85)	Entren _____ ed	197)	Snap _____ ot
86)	Ran _____	198)	_____ ame
87)	Pari _____	199)	_____ aff
88)	Spla _____	200)	_____ udder
89)	Tickli _____	201)	Ca _____ ew
90)	Distingui _____ ed	202)	Ravi _____ ing
91)	_____ aft	203)	Crun _____
92)	Ar _____ duke	204)	_____ ift
93)	_____ earful	205)	Staun _____
94)	Avalan _____ e	206)	_____ erubim
95)	Me _____	207)	Flouri _____
96)	_____ arred	208)	_____ artered
97)	Haberda _____ er	209)	_____ ould
98)	_____ abby	210)	Book _____ elves
99)	_____ eap	211)	Bra _____ ly
100)	Angui _____	212)	_____ arity
101)	En _____ anted	213)	_____ ell-
102)	_____ rouded		_____ ocked
103)	_____ uckle	214)	Har _____
104)	Ostri _____ es	215)	_____ inked
105)	Vou _____ er	216)	_____ ilean
106)	Sma _____ ing	217)	_____ oal
107)	_____ erry	218)	_____ anting

108)	Astoni _____ ing	**219)**	_____ amberlain
109)	_____ elter	**220)**	_____ ipped tooth
110)	_____ ared	**221)**	Langui _____
111)	_____ arming	**222)**	Ex _____ equer
112)	Thre _____ old	**223)**	_____ eri _____

RIGHT or WRITE and MORE

Choose the correct word to complete the sentence.

1) Raise your _____ hand and repeat after me.
a) write
b) right

2) The _____ question is: are they ready to collaborate with us?
a) reel
b) real

3) The coach is the man with the _____ whistle.
a) read
b) red

4) _____ late!
a) Your
b) You're

5) The coach is asking _____ the driver is ready to take the team to the stadium.
a) whether
b) weather

134

6) There will be a new _____ appointed to this college.
a) principle
b) principal

7) He had a _____ red T-Shirt on.
a) plane
b) plain

8) _____ car is parked in the driveway?
a) Who's
b) Whose

9) See you _____!
a) there
b) they're
c) their

10) _____ is absolutely nothing to do in this town!
a) There
b) They're
c) Their

11) _____ the people who are buying the company.
a) There
b) They're
c) Their

12) The children miss you _____.
a) to
b) too

13)
- The mailman brought these letters _____ you.
a) four
b) for

- When?
- _____ hours ago.
a) To
b) Two
c) Too

14) We are going shopping: I need a new _____ of jeans.
a) pear
b) pair

15) They wasted precious time in _____ talks.
a) idol
b) idle

16) We have _____ the competition for the second time.
a) one
b) won

17) The labourers couldn't afford to _____ the money they had worked hard _____.
a) waist/waste
b) for/four

18) We are working at changing the fact that the staff is mostly _____ at the moment.
a) mail
b) male

19) Use the gloves. It's dangerous to operate this machine with your _____ hands.
a) bear
b) bare

20) Enjoy your _____! It smells delicious, by the way.
a) mill
b) meal

21) Those chairs are made of _____.
a) would
b) wood

22) Her medical condition has made Jessica quite _____.
a) week
b) weak

23) The new building _____ can accommodate twenty homes.
a) site
b) sight

24) _____ will be more appropriate for the buildings.
a) Steal
b) Steel

25) Where can _____ _____ some stamps?
a) Eye, I
b) bye, buy, by

26) The phone can't work without _____ battery.
a) its
b) it's

27) When is your _____'s birthday?
a) sun
b) son

28) They are going to _____ at noon.
a) meat
b) meet

29) After she lost the _____, the queen was _____ in jail.
a) thrown, throne
b) throne, thrown

30) The neighbourhood is off limits because it is a crime
_____.
a) seen
b) scene

31) There is _____ room here _____ the furniture.
a) no
b) know
c) four
d) for

32) Reading _____ can be fun and very useful.
a) aloud
b) allowed

33) The deadline is the end of this _____.
a) weak
b) week

34) This has _____ an important meeting.
a) bean
b) been

35) Maggie will travel across the Red _____ to Egypt.
a) See
b) Sea

36) I had a _____ jab before I _____ to Kenya.
a) flu, flew
b) flu, flew

37) They are meeting in half an _____.
a) our
b) hour

38) Throw it in the _____.
a) been
b) bin
c) bean

39) The winner will get a gold _____.
a) meddle
b) medal

40) Have you ever _____ this movie before?
a) seen
b) scene

41) Let's _____ what they have to say.
a) here
b) hear

42) A severed _____ could result in a serious hemorrhage.
a) vein
b) vain

43) The wind _____ her hat off.
a) blue
b) blew

44) _____ your raincoat: it's pouring outside.
a) Wear
b) Where

45) _____ are you?
a) Wear
b) Where

46) His family will _____ miss his wedding for the world!
a) knot
b) not

47) They traveled over mountains and _____ to be with their family.
a) sees
b) seas

48) She brought you a _____ of chocolate cake.
a) peace
b) piece

49) _____ of the new books will be allocated to senior students.
a) Sum
b) Some

50) The house will sell for at _____ three millions.
a) leased
b) least

51) The secretary has _____ your email.
a) read
b) red

52) The parcel was _____ from Norway.
a) cent
b) sent

53)
The _____ left the camp early this morning.
a) night
b) knight

He will be back at _____.
a) knight
b) night

54) How much _____ do you need for the cake?
a)   flower
b)   flour

55) Is feminine of 'monk'; _____?
a)   none
b)   nun

56) Does your _____ still live in New Jersey?
a)   ant
b)   aunt

57) The children prefer _____ for breakfast.
a)   serial
b)   cereal

58) How is your _____ friend doing?
a)   deer
b)   dear

59) All the climbers were aiming for the _____ of the mountain.
a)   peek
b)   peak

60) Making it this far in this grammar and vocabulary manual is such an impressive _____.
a)   feet
b)   feat

61) Who _____ how to fix a computer?
a)   nose
b)   knows

62)

- Samia hurt her _____ in the fall.
a) heal
b) heel

- How long will it take to _____?
a) heel
b) heal

63) The dog had its _____ caught in the door.
a) tale
b) tail

64) The lift is out of order. Please take the _____.
a) stares
b) stairs

65) If you really want to help, _____ the cheese.
a) grate
b) great

66) There's a _____ on at the mall: you can now get the shoes you wanted.
a) sail
b) sale

67) Those _____ are powered by the wind.
a) meals
b) mills

68) This is a mosquito _____!
a) byte
b) bite

69) A heavy _____ might cause floods.
a) reign
b) rain

70) The _____ is the reason we have honey.
a) be
b) bee

71) She owes her great looks to good _____.
a) jeans
b) genes

72) _____ the cream in the bowl.
a) Poor
b) Pour

73) The waiting time can _____ between 10 to 15 minutes.
a) very
b) vary

74)
    When can we have a _____? I am starving!
a) break
b) brake

    I'll have a _____ pizza!
a) hole
b) whole

75) They make documentaries about birds of _____.
a) prey
b) pray

76) She _____ _____ in her _____ that it was the right thing to do.
a) new
b) knew
c) deep
d) dip
e) sole
f) soul

77) These coats are on _____.
a) sail
b) sale

78) Remember to buy some _____.
a) bred
b) bread

79) Long _____ is not always convenient.
a) hare
b) hair

80) The president and his family had to _____ the country after the military coup.
a) flea
b) flee

81) The senator will meet and _____ the local business leaders.
a) grit
b) greet

82) It's rude to _____.
a) stair
b) stare

83) Rita _____ all the answers.
a) new
b) knew

84) Check the closet. There is a _____ in there. This floor needs sweeping.
a) bloom
b) broom
c) balloon

85) The list of the candidate is on the _____.
a) bored
b) board

86) You are all _____ to leave the room.
a) aloud
b) allowed

87) The Sheriff _____ in town on a magnificent _____.
a) road, rode
b) horse, hoarse

88) The prisoner had his _____ behind his back.
a) ends
b) hands

They were _____ behind his back.
c) tied
d) tide

89) Let's all work hard at _____ this deals.
a) ceiling
b) sealing

90) The _____ keeps the house cleaned.
a) made
b) maid

91) Sir, what is the difference between tablets and _____?
a) bills
b) pills

92) The _____ departed from LAX.
a) plain
b) plane

93) They will need more _____ for the _____.
a) wool
b) wood
c) file
d) fire

94) How long is going to be in _____ after his wife's death?
a) mourning
b) morning

94) Driving on icy _____ can be dangerous.
a) loads
b) roads

95) The organisers are asking _____ or not Smart-Tech will attend the exhibition.
a) weather
b) whether

96) The wind _____ all morning.
a) blue
b) blew

97) Raoul bought his wife a diamond _____.
a) wring
b) ring

98) Our country played an important _____ in the resolution of the conflict.
a)   roll
b)   role

99) You must keep _____ in the library.
a)   quite
b)   quit
c)   quiet

100) The train _____ is £25.
a)   fair
b)   fare

101) The children had cheesecake for _____.
a)   desert
b)   dessert

102) Is _____ the same as corn?
a)   maze
b)   maize

103) As _____ to the throne, he has very important duties.
a)   air
b)   heir

104) To loose _____, you can go on a diet and also exercise.
a)   wait
b)   weight

105) Ali _____ the office's address.
a)   knows
b)   nose

106) For this recipe, the chef needs to buy more garlic and _____.
a) thyme
b) time

107) The _____ base is out of town.
a) navel
b) naval
c) novel

108) All the equipment is _____; _____ the amplifier.
a) ear
b) hear
c) here
d) exempt
e) expect
f) except

109) This is the best market to get _____ fruit and vegetables.
a) flesh
b) fresh

110) The packet could _____ three kilograms.
a) way
b) weigh

111) The _____ and the roof need repairing.
a) sailing
b) ceiling

112) The minister will be held accountable for all the _____ he has been leaking to the _____.
a) staff
b) stuff
c) price
d) press

113) The bomb squad _____ the device.
a) defused
b) diffused

114) There's a _____ in the roof. The room could be flooded if it's not fixed at once.
a) leek
b) leak

115) They will be here on _____.
a) Sundae
b) Sunday

116) The _____ thing is that you secured that lucrative contract.
a) mane
b) main

117) The trainees left the room _____ together.
a) hole
b) whole
c) all
d) alt

118) The companies _____ accepting any more applications.
a) aunt
b) aren't

119) Their grandmother can't hear you: she is _____.
a) death
b) deaf

120) Let's add some _____ to the vegetables.
a) meet
b) meat

121) The main offices are located in the _____ city.
a)   capitol
b)   capital

122) Regina bought some _____ for her hair.
a)   die
b)   dye

123) Anita bought some _____ apples.
a)   read
b)   red

124) _____ can we find a vegetarian restaurant?
a)   Where
b)   Wear

125) The children have _____ so much!
a)   groan
b)   grown

126) Our brave soldiers invaded and took _____ the country!
a)   oval
b)   over

127) The swimmer was swept out to sea by the _____.
a)   tied
b)   tide

128) You need to take your _____: it is freezing outside.
a)   cloves
b)   gloves

129) The _____ here can be quite unpredictable.
a)   weather
b)   whether

130) The extreme _____ caused the _____ of all the crops.
a) it
b) heat
c) death
d) deaf

131) Please, can you _____ this application form and sign it?
a) feel
b) fill

132) The tourist was stung by a _____.
a) bee
b) be

133) Don't drink from the bottle. Could you use a _____?
a) class
b) glass

134) The players will be _____ on the field after halftime.
a) pack
b) back

135) What makes you say that 'Life isn't _____'?
a) fare
b) fair

136) Raoul Jobs and Bill Dale _____ that company early 1990s.
a) confounded
b) cofounded

137) Our aunt paid the water, electricity, phone and gas
    _____.
a) pills
b) tills
c) bills

138) The _____ of this boot is made _____ rubber.
a) soul
b) sole
c) off
d) of

139) Mrs. Brown is a _____. She flies airplanes.
a) pirate
b) pilot

140) Studying English _____ and vocabulary can support
    our reading, writing, listening and speaking.
a) glamour
b) grammar

141) After he had been completely _____, the suspect
    finally _____ to the police.
a) surrendered
b) surrounded

142) The _____ Family will get together for Her Majesty's
    birthday.
a) Royal
b) Loyal

143) There is a free _____ here. I promise to _____ it
    for you, so that we can _____ together.
a) safe
b) save
c) sit
d) seat

144) One hundred metres; that's the _____ of this part of the river.
a) deaf
b) depth
c) death

145) The neighbours are going _____ this weekend.
a) boring
b) bowling

146) There were large _____ on the streets to welcome the World Champions.
a) clouds
b) crowds

147) Only tick the _____ answers.
a) light
b) right

148) This is where they _____ the organic vegetables!
a) glow
b) grow

149) The plane will _____ at noon.
a) alive
b) arrive

150) The book is so _____ it can be used _____ a pillow!
a) sick
b) thick
c) has
d) as

151) This is none of your business. So, you might as well keep your _____ shut!
a) mouse
b) mouth

152) The bride and the _____ have known each other since high school.
a) groom
b) gloom

153) You'll need a _____ for those roses.
a) phase
b) vase

154) That was a _____ entertaining event.
a) fairy
b) very

155) The book has been receiving great _____.
a) reviews
b) refuse

156) A _____ field has been set aside out of town for the new university.
a) fast
b) vast

157) Donald rented a _____ in order to move his belongings to his new house.
a) fan
b) van

158) Is the polar _____ an endangered species?
a) bare
b) bear

159) The _____ that the taylor made to your suit make it look much better.
a) alterations
b) alternatives

160) Linda needs to take the boots back to the store and ask for a refund. She will need her _____.
a)   resit
b)   receipt

161) That river was not deep enough for anyone to actually _____ in it!
a)   drowse
b)   drown

162) I can't wait for the summer _____!
a)   sails
b)   sales

I need new shoes, socks, T-shirts and so on.
I will buy myself some brand new _____.
a)   clothes
b)   cloths

163) Here is your change. Three £10 _____.
a)   pills
b)   bills

164) I _____ it doesn't _____ tomorrow.
a)   prey
b)   play
c)   pray
d)   reign
e)   rain

165) The store is quite busy.
We need more staff on the _____.
a)   tells
b)   tills

166) You don't have to be _____ to play basketball.
a)   toll
b)   tall
c)   tool
d)   stool

167) Disobey this library's rules; and there will be some very serious _____!
a)   repercussions
b)   concussion
c)   precautions
d)   consequent

168) Even more work is required _____ the next _____.
a)   to rich
b)   to reach
c)   libel
d)   level
e)   label

169) It's _____ your team is not qualified for the World Cup.
a)   ashamed
b)   a shame

170) The hurricane left a trail of _____.
a)   distraction
b)   destruction

171) The instructors are training the students to leave their desks and classrooms _____ and tidy.
a)   meat
b)   neat

172) Marilyn is such an accomplished musician. She can play the _____ very well.
a) hard
b) dart
c) harp

173) What do you want to watch: a _____ show or an action movie?
a) comedy
b) comely

174)
- What did you _____ the children?
- I only informed them that the party was cancelled.
a) well
b) sell
c) tell
d) bell

175) After their long and busy days, the children were so exhausted that they are now sound _____.
a) sleep
b) asleep

176) Their cousin is getting married; and of course, they all didn't really need an invitation to the _____.
a) weeding
b) wedding

177)
- How does your little brother like his birthday gifts?
- Judging by the huge _____ on his face, he must like them a lot!
a) green
b) grin

178) After working in the fields for hours, the farmers' energy level began to _____.
a) win
b) wane

179) £250! That's too much. I can't let you pay that all by yourself. Please, let's _____ the bill.
a) spill
b) spell
c) spit
d) split
e) spin

180) We've got an early start tomorrow.
   I'm going to _____.
a) bad
b) bet
c) bed
d) bite
e) bit

   I _____ you do the same.
a) recommence
b) accommodate
c) recommend
d) investigate

181) They say 'practice makes perfect'. A little effort each day can help us _____ more vocabulary and grammar, in order to become more competent and fluent in English.
a) muster
b) master

182) After the rain, there was _____ all around the house.
a) mad
b) mud

183) The recipe says '_____ the vegetables in the _____; _____ do not add any water for half an hour'.
a) but
b) pot
c) put
d) bot

184) After she retires, Nadia plans to travel around the _____.
a) word
b) world

185) _____ Nadia travel by boat or by plane?
a) Will
b) Wheel

186) These flowers _____ to grow only in summer.
a) tend
b) send

187) Pedro now works as an investment _____ for a Mexican multinational.
a) bunker
b) banker

188) The Smith family spent a month travelling across the _____.
a) jingle
b) jungle

189) You can go ahead. I will join you at the restaurant as soon as I am done. I _____ have this report to finish.
a) steal
b) still

190) The architect and the property developers are touring the new building _____.
a) sit
b) sat
c) site
d) sight
e) side
f) sigh

191) Is the silver back _____ an endangered species?
a) guerilla
b) gorilla

192) These were extremely sensitive matters; so the committee had to _____ carefully.
a) thread
b) tread

193) The sheer _____ of information about what actually took place further complicated the entire enquiry.
a) death
b) dearth

194) The disgruntled employees decided to lodge an official _____.
a) complain
b) complaint

PAST PARTICIPLE or VERB 3

Present perfect
Put the verb in brackets in the *present* perfect tense.
Hint: You will need the past participle or verb 3.

1) I (never, to be) to Bali.

_____

2) Raoul (always, to do) his work well.

_____

3) She (not, always, to arrive) on time.

_____

4) Why you (not, to call) the police yet?

_____

5) It feels like we (to know) each other for decades.

_____

Past perfect
Put the verb in brackets in the *past* perfect tense.
Hint: You will need the past participle or verb 3.

1) The party (not, to start) when we arrived.

_____

2) The manager (already, to leave) for his conference when the news broke.

_____

3) It was such a relief to hear that my suitcase (to arrive) on the following flight.

_____

4) If John (not, to break) his leg, he would have been on tour with all the other players.

_____

5) There (to be) a wedding next door; so Musab didn't have a good night sleep.

_____

6) They weren't going to be allowed back in, to attend to meeting if they (not, to apologise).

_____

7) If their car (not, to be) clamped, Isaac and Teresa wouldn't have taken a taxi.

_____

8) Her colleagues invited Miriam to lunch, but she (already, to eat).

_____

9) As soon as Lauren realised that she (not, to lock) her front door, she ran back home.

_____

10) Ahmed is confident he would not have enjoyed working overseas if he (to accept) that job in Argentina.

_____

11) If I (to be) you, I would have asked to speak with the manager.

_____

12) The harvest was not great because it (not, to rain) for months.

_____

13) He (already, to have) sold-out concerts by the time he could even vote!

_____

14) Remy and Rita couldn't believe their friends (to travel) from Australia to Newcastle to be at their wedding!

_____

15) Before Mr. Johnson showed us the pictures of his trip to South America; Argentina and Mexico (never, to be) on our To Go Places list.

_____

16) *The Matrix* and *Avatar* were the most amazing movies Greg (ever, to see).

_____

17) Ade (never, to be) to Manchester before he got a job there.

_____

18) It (to rain, *Progressive or Continuous form*) heavily for months; and that eventually caused the dam to break.

_____

19) If the window (not, to leave open, *Passive Voice*); the burglar would certainly never have been able to get into the house.

_____

_____

20) Aisha (to be) living in Canada for seven years, when her parents came to visit her.

_____

Future perfect

Put the verb in brackets in the *future* perfect tense.
Hint: You will need the past participle or verb 3.

1) The team will (to complete) the basic tasks by the time you arrive.

_____

2) The meeting will (not, to end) then.

_____

3) This time next year, we will (to be) in business for eighteen years!

_____

4) Will the workers (to finish) all the plumbing by September?

_____

5) They will (to graduate) by now.

_____

Passive voice
Put the sentences in the corresponding passive voice.
Hint: You will need the past participle or verb 3.

Present simple

Samiah cooks dinner.	
The students clean the rooms.	
The class leader reads the names.	
The teacher writes the date.	

Past simple

Samiah cooked dinner.	
The students cleaned the rooms.	
The class leader read the names.	
The teacher wrote the date.	

Present progressive or continuous

Samiah is cooking dinner.	
The students are cleaning the rooms.	
The class leader is reading the names.	
The teacher is writing the date.	

Past progressive or continuous

Samiah was cooking dinner.	
The students were cleaning the rooms.	
The class leader was reading the names.	
The teacher was writing the date.	

Present perfect

Put the sentences on the left in **present perfect tense.**

Write the *passive voice* of each of the **present perfect** sentences.

Hint 1: You will need the past participle or verb 3 in both tasks.

Hint 2: For the passive voice, you will also use the auxiliary *been*.

Samiah cooks dinner.	

The students clean the rooms.	
The class leader reads the names.	
The teacher writes the date.	

'to be **going to...**' for **future** plans

Samiah is going to cook dinner.	Dinner is going _____ Samiah.
The students are going to clean the rooms.	
The class leader is going to read the names.	
The teacher is going to write the date.	
Selim is going to borrow Yisham's car.	

Future simple

Put the sentences on the left in **future simple tense.**

Write the *passive voice* of each of the **future simple** sentences.

Hint 1: You will need the modal *will* for each of the future simple sentences.

Hint 2: You will need both the modal *will and* the past participle for each of the passive voice sentences.

Samiah cooks dinner.	
The students clean the rooms.	
The class leader reads the names.	
The teacher writes the date.	

Future perfect

Put the sentences on the left in **future perfect tense.**

Write the *passive voice* of each of the **future perfect** sentences.

Hint 1: You will need the modal *will* for each of the future perfect sentences.

Hint 2: You will need both the modal *will and* the past participle for each of the passive voice sentences; as well as the auxiliary *been.*

Samiah cooks dinner.	
The students clean the rooms.	
The class leader reads the names.	
The teacher writes the date.	

Reported Speech
Put the sentences on the left in corresponding **reported speech.**

Past simple	Present perfect
"I found your keys", the security guard said.	
"I took your order", the waitress told me.	
"We spoke with your parents at the meeting", the teachers informed us.	

Put the sentences on the left in present perfect tense and then write each corresponding past perfect **reported speech.**

Present perfect	Past perfect
"I found your keys", the security guard said.	
"I took your order", the waitress told me.	

"We spoke with your parents at the meeting", the teachers informed us.	

Had I ... *instead of* **If** (Third Conditional)
Put the verb in brackets in the correct tense.

Hint 1: You will need the *past perfect* tense.
Hint 2: You will need either *could* or *would*.
        1) is an example.

1) The player (to score) that goal, his team would have won the game.
- *Had the player scored the goal, his team would have won the game.*

2) Had Lisa told her parents she had made other arrangements, they (not, to tidy up) her bedroom.

3) You (to text) us in time, we could have picked you up from the train station.

4) The rain (to fall) as normal, the farmers would have had good harvests.

5) Had she campaigned diligently, Senator O'Malley (to be) reelected.

6) Maurice (to wake up) early, he would be on the bus with his classmates.

7) They (to know) that Dr. Proust would be such a great congresswoman; Terry and his family would have voted for her.

ALREADY, ANYMORE, NO LONGER, STILL, YET

Choose the correct word to complete the sentence.

1) Yuki _____ lives in Seattle. She moved back to Kyoto last month.

2) He doesn't like that car _____.
He is _____ buying a new one!

3)
- Have you met André _____?
- Yes. The secretary has _____ introduced him to the team.

4) Does your committee _____ need more time to complete the presentation?

5) He doesn't want to talk to you _____!
What are you _____ doing here?

6) The contractor does _____ require our services.

7) Ron's crew has _____ met their target.

8) Is dinner ready _____?

9)
- Do you care for a bowl of soup?
- No. Thank you. I _____ ate.

10) Why hasn't the shop _____ delivered the tools?

AND, BUT, OR, SO

Choose the correct word to complete the sentence.

1) They parked _____ found a good restaurant for lunch.
2) Ameer had no cash, _____ he used his debit card.
3) Arun was late _____ he still took his time.
4) Do you want a pizza _____ a burger for dinner?
5) We are buying fruit _____ vegetables.
6) They wanted to call you _____ they didn't have any time.
7) He is either going to be reelected _____ lose his seat in parliament.
8) He arrived late, _____ she missed the beginning of the lecture.

ALTHOUGH/THOUGH/EVEN THOUGH, FOR, BECAUSE, YET

Choose the correct word to complete the sentence.

1) You passed your exam _____ you work very hard.
2) _____ Sajeed was unwell, he still came to class.
3) The floor is flooded, _____ the door was left open.
4) They are putting on weight _____ they stopped exercising and eating healthy.
5) These students have an important exam, _____ they aren't reviewing.
6) _____ they left home early, they missed the bus.
7) The dogs are excited, _____ the children are back from school.
8) I have said sorry several times, _____ he won't take my calls!

USE, USED, USED TO, USE TO

Choose the correct word to complete the sentence.

1)
- My cousin *used to/use to* live in Germany. He has now moved to Portugal.
- Who *used to/use to* live in Canada then?
2) Where did the neighbours *used to/use to* work?
3) Dr. Norman *used/use* the auditorium for a conference.
4)
- Why did your uncle *used to/use to* run for hours?
- He was training for a marathon.
5) What did you *used to/use to* do? How did you *used to/use to* spend your weekends?
6) In college, they *used to/use to* spend the weekend at the library preparing for their exams.

7) The policeman *used/use* his baton to break the window and save the child.
8) When do we *used/use* the green room?
9) What *used to/use to* be on these lands?
   Who *used to/use to* own them?
10) How did the children *used to/use to* go to school?
11) Why didn't they *used/use* all that space?
12) Who *used to/use to* rent this apartment?
13) When are you going to *used /use* the money you have been saving for years?
14) Did Dr. Jones *used to/use to* be in the Navy?
15) Where did your parents *used to/use to* buy fish?
16)
- Did you *used/use* all of the shampoo?
- No, I only *used/use* a little.
17) Who just *used/use* this computer?
18) The beautiful sights *used to/use to* attract many tourists.
19) It *used to/use to* rain a lot here.
20) Which sports did you *used to/use to* like as a child?

IRREGULAR and **REGULAR VERBS**: a few examples

Complete the table with the corresponding verbs.

Verb	Past Simple	Past Participle
		burnt/burned
		dreamt/dreamed
		learnt/learned
	smelt/smelled	
	spelt/spelled	
	bet/betted	
		leant/leaned
		leapt/leaped
		lit/lighted
		quit/quitted
		spilt/spilled
		spoilt/spoiled
	foiled	
fall		
feel		
fill		
leave		
found		
	brought	
	bought	
	caught	
	fought	
	taught	
	thought	
		burst
		cast
		cost
		cut
		hit
		hurt
		let

		put
		quit
		read
		set
		shed
		shut
		split
		spread
cook		
play		
watch		
study		
clean		
wash		
touch		
	was, were	
	came	
		beaten
		bitten
		broken
		chosen
		driven
		eaten
		forgiven
		forgotten
		frozen
		given
see		
	hid	
	rode	
	rose	
	shook	
	stole	
	swelled	
		taken
	woke	

		written
	had	
	kept	
		blown
		flown
		grown
		known
		thrown
		worn
	won	
	made	
	copied	
	paid	
ring		
say		
sleep		
sit	spoke	
	spent	
sweep		
		swum
lose		
	heard	
hold		
kneel		
lend		
	drank	
	find	
	did	
	met	
tell		
	realised	
	used	
go		
	stayed	
attend		

	occupied	
	explained	
delay		
	started	
	look	
	ran	
remember		

COMPARATIVE and SUPERLATIVE ADJECTIVES

Complete the table with the corresponding adjectives.

Adjective	Comparative	Superlative
beautiful		
expensive		
important		
tiny		
bad		
	farther or further	
good		
big		
fat		
mad		
fit		
wet		
hot		
thin		
		fastest
	flattest	
	dimmer	
	hipper	
	sadder	
	gladder	
busy		
easy		
pretty		

LANGUAGE, NATIONALITY and COUNTRY

Complete the table with the corresponding word.

Language	Nationality	Country
		Brazil
	Spanish	
Danish		
		France
Japanese		
	Egyptian	
Hungarian		
		Oman
	Togolese	
		Portugal
	Iraqi	
	Jordanian	
		Australia
		Turkey
		Vietnam
Greek		
	Mexican	
	Ghanaian	
German		
	Chinese	
	Angolese	
Finnish		
Norwegian		
		United Kingdom
	Bahraini	

WHAT TIME IS IT?

Draw the hands of the clock to show the time.

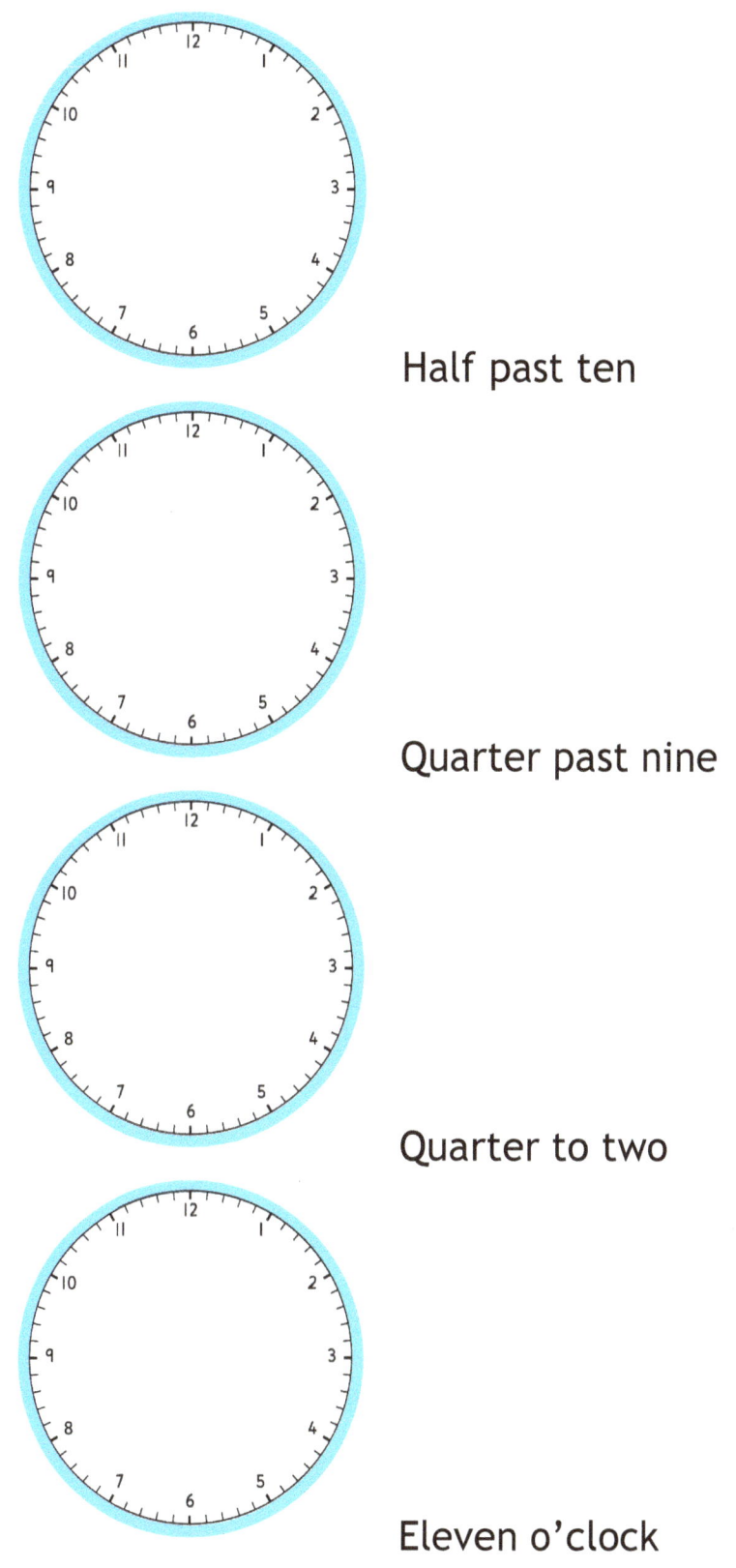

Half past ten

Quarter past nine

Quarter to two

Eleven o'clock

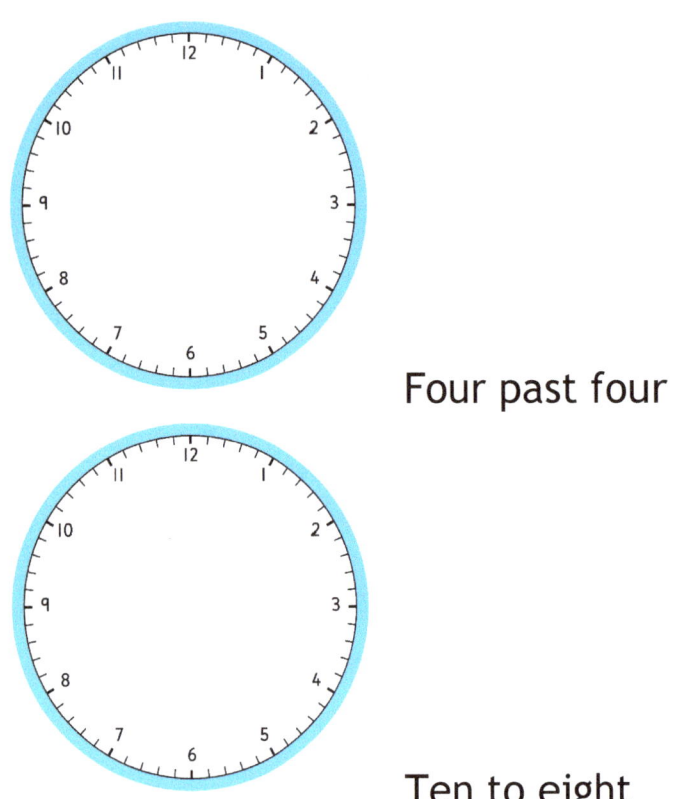

Four past four

Ten to eight

FAMILY TREE

Complete the sentence with the correct word from the list below.

> uncle, husband, brother-in-law, nephew, son,
> niece, sisters, cousins, wife, daughter, aunt,
> grandmother, stepmother, half-sisters, sister-in-
> law, wife, great-grandmother, ex-wife

1) Joanna had a baby. He is a boy. His name is Richard.
   He's Joanna's _____.

2) Joanna and Camilla have the same father, Donavan.
   Joanna and Camilla are _____.
   Camilla is married to Jonathan. He is Joanna's _____.
   Camilla is Jonathan's _____.
   Joanna and Camilla are actually _____, as they don't
   have the same mother.

3) Camilla and Joanna's father has a brother, Kevin and a
   sister, Becky.
   Kevin is Camilla and Joanna's _____.
   Becky is Camilla and Joanna's _____.

4) Kevin is no longer married to Alexandra. They had a
   divorce five years ago. Alexandra is Kevin's _____.
   Kevin used to be Alexandra's _____.
   They have a _____ called Michelle.

5) Camilla, Joanna and Michelle are all _____.

6) Camilla and Jonathan had fraternal twins: Simon and
   Teresa.
   Simon is Joanna's _____.
   Teresa is Joanna's _____.

7) Kevin remarried last month. His new _____ is Chloe.
   Chloe is Michelle's _____.

8) Donavan, Kevin and Becky are planning a party for their
   mother, Shirley's birthday.
   Shirley is Camilla, Becky, and Michelle's _____.
   Shirley is Simon, Teresa and Richard's _____.

SO and SUCH

Choose the correct word to complete the sentence.

1) The new president is *so/such* eloquent and charismatic.
2) It is *so/such* an absolute pleasure to finally get to meet you!
3) Rasheed is *so/such* a character!
4) The show ended *so/such* fast.
5) The place was *so/such* crowded we could barely even move.
6) The captain played *so/such* well, he won his team the game.
7) You are *so/such* a nerd.
8) It was *so/such* a memorable event; I will always cherish it.

COMPARATIVE and SUPERLATIVE ADJECTIVES

Choose the correct word to complete the sentence.

1)
- Lesson 4 isn't _____.
a) the difficult
b) the most challenging
c) the more difficult

- In actuality, Lesson 4 is _____ than Lessons 1, 2 and 3.
a) easy
b) easiest
c) simpler
d) the tricky

2) _____ moment is the book is when the two brothers left their friends and headed to boarding school.
a) Sad
b) Sadder
c) The saddest

3) We need more light here. Why is this room so _____?
a) dim
b) dimmer
c) dimmest
d) the darkest

4)
- Helena looks _____ now. Has she been exercising?
a) thinner
b) thinnest
c) fittest
d) the healthiest

- This is also the _____ she's ever been!
a) happy
b) happier
c) happiest
d) the happiest

5) Are poisonous snakes _____ than scorpions?
a) most dangerous
b) the most dangerous
c) deadliest
d) more lethal

6) Gomez is _____ player of the team this season.
a) fitter
b) the fittest
c) the fiddler

7) Winning the lottery was _____ day of Anita's life!
a) good
b) the best
c) worse
d) excellent

8) The prince owns _____ yacht in the world.
a) more expensive
b) the more expensive
c) the most luxurious
d) better than

9) Is today _____ than yesterday?
a) hottest
b) the hottest
c) hot
d) hotter
e) hot hot

10) Beverly Castle is _____ than Ocean Palace.
a) cheap
b) cheapest
c) cheaper than
d) cheaper

11) This option is the _____ they are ever going to get.
a) good
b) better
c) best
d) the best

12) So far, this season has been _____ this year.
a) the wettest
b) wetter than
c) fatter than
d) wetter

13) By far, the _____ intelligent student in the class is you!
a) more
b) most
c) the most
d) cleverest

14) The baby's skin rash looks _____ than yesterday.
a) radish
b) red
c) redder
d) reddest

15) Ladies and Gentlemen, we present to you _____ TV screen in the world!
a) flat
b) flatter
c) the flatter
d) the flattest

16) Put it back in the oven. The dish should be much _____ than this.
a) ready
b) red
c) redder
d) the reddest

CONTRACTIONS

What does the contraction (*in italics*) stand for?

1) *We'll* see about that.
a) We would
b) We need to
c) We will
d) We shall not

2) *Who's* got the key to the store room?
a) Who is
b) Who has
c) Whose
d) Who should

3) The meeting *mustn't* be cancelled.
a) mustard
b) must note
c) must never
d) must not

4) *Who's* responsible for all this mess?
a) Who has
b) Whose
c) Who is
d) Who should

5) That village *can't* be reached at present because of the torrential rains.
a) cans
b) can
c) cannot
d) couldn't

6) *She's* the deputy director.
a) She has
b) She is
c) She had
d) She was

7) *She's* been very patient.
a) She is
b) She had
c) She has
d) She hasn't

8) The election *wasn't* last month.
a) was never
b) has never
c) was not
d) has not

9) *We'll* be there.
a) We will
b) We would
c) We should
d) Will

11) Audrey *didn't* turn in the homework.
a) don't
b) does not
c) doesn't
d) did not

12) Pedro *hasn't* arrived yet.
a) had not
b) has
c) has not
d) hasn't had

13) Peter and his cousins *aren't* on the bus.
a) are not
b) have not
c) haven't
d) ants

14) *That'll* never fail.
a) That should
b) That would
c) That would have
d) That will

15) That *won't* happen!
a) would
b) would not
c) will not
d) wouldn't

16) *It's* time to conclude the conference.
a) It is
b) It has
c) It had
d) It shall

17) Two cars *wouldn't* suffice.
a) will not
b) would not
c) shouldn't
d) should not

18) *You'd* better pass the test this time!
a) You would
b) You are
c) You had
d) You have

19) *They've* broken a new world record.
a)   They had
b)   They have
c)   They are
d)   They have not

20) *Where's* the receipt?
a)   Where is
b)   Where has
c)   Where are
d)   Where hasn't

21) *I'd* like to speak with the manager, please.
a)   I shouldn't
b)   I would
c)   I will
d)   I had

22) *Let's* start.
a)   Let has
b)   Let us
c)   Let is
d)   Let have

23) *That's* all Leon told us.
a)   That has
b)   That is
c)   That isn't
d)   That has not

24) *You're* welcome.
a)   You have
b)   You are
c)   You hadn't
d)   You haven't

25)   Carol *shouldn't* take too long.
a)   should not
b)   shall not
c)   should not have
d)   could not

26) *I'm* ready.
a)   I am
b)   I have
c)   I am not
d)   I must

27) Samia *hasn't* seen the new office.
a)   had not
b)   will not
c)   has not
d)   hadn't

28) *I'll* be right back.
a)   I should
b)   I will
c)   I would
d)   I shan't

29) They *don't* have the authority.
a)   do
b)   do not
c)   doesn't
d)   does not

30) Ester and Aisha *haven't* missed a single class.
a)   have never
b)   have note
c)   have not
d)   hadn't

31) *What's* the matter?
a)   What is
b)   What has
c)   What was
d)   What has not

32) *We'd* taken our time on this very serious matter.
a)   We had
b)   We should
c)   We could
d)   We don't

33) *I'd* rather improve my English.
a)   I had
b)   I would
c)   I shouldn't
d)   I do

34) *How's* work?
a)   How was
b)   How is
c)   How has
d)   How isn't

35) The elections *weren't* free, fair and transparent.
a)   were not
b)   haven't
c)   hadn't
d)   will not

36) *Who's* he?
a)   Whose
b)   Who is
c)   Who has
d)   Who had

37) The ministers *couldn't* attend this gathering today.
a) could not
b) shouldn't
c) cannot
d) could never

38) It *isn't* exactly what happened.
a) is not
b) has not
c) hasn't
d) had not

39) No. They *haven't* been cooperating.
a) has not
b) have not
c) have never
d) had not had

40) *You'll* be held accountable.
a) You have
b) You won't
c) You will
d) You shall not

41) The farmers *aren't* living the rice fields.
a) are not
b) haven't
c) have not
d) had not
e) is not

42) The students *weren't* aware of the change of schedule.
a) was not
b) wear
c) were not
d) worn out

43) Tom, *there's* a phone call for you.
a) there has
b) there was
c) is there
d) there is

44) *That's* the house the driver was talking about.
a) That is
b) That was
c) That has
d) That is not

45) *Where's* the new computer?
a) Where has
b) Where was
c) Where is
d) There is

46) *Who'll* find out the plumber's number?
a) Who would
b) Who shall not
c) Who will
d) Who won't

IDIOMS: a tiny introductory list

1 - Match each idiom to its meaning.

Example: 5c – To hit the books. = To study hard.

1	Let the cat out of the bag.	He got treated the way he's been treating others.	a
2	To have a bun in the oven.	To be extremely expensive.	b
3	I am all ears.	**To study hard.**	c
4	Get a taste of his own medicine.	You are not talented at this.	d
5	**To hit the books.**	To be unwell.	e
6	To be under the weather.	To be pregnant	f
7	To cost an arm and a leg.	To tell a secret.	g
8	Don't give your day job.	Tell me more.	h

2 - Match each idiom to its meaning.

1	To beat around the bush.	An easy target.	a
2	Let's call it a day!	A lenient punishment.	b
3	A sitting duck.	To be upset.	c
4	To give someone the cold shoulder.	To refuse to acknowledge the truth.	d
5	To turn a blind eye.	Avoid getting to the point.	e
6	To be bent out of shape.	A favourable situation which wasn't or didn't appear so initially.	f
7	A blessing in disguise	Bring our day's work to a close.	g
8	A slap on the wrist.	To ignore someone.	h

THE ENGLISH ALPHABET

Complete with the missing letters.

	B	C		E	F	
H		J				N
O	P				T	U
	W		Z			

THE DAYS OF THE WEEK

Unscramble the names.
Note: The *first letter* **must** be a capital letter.

amyodn   _____

hsayurtd   _____

eatusyd   _____

auynds   _____

tyduasar   _____

fadyir   _____

asenddywe   _____

Put the days of the week in the correct order.
1 –
2 –
3 –
4 –
5 –
6 –
7 -

THE MONTHS OF THE YEAR

Find the 12 months of the year.

Months

F	J	R	N	O	C	T	O	B	E	R	I	F	E
O	U	M	S	E	P	T	E	M	B	E	R	C	J
P	L	R	N	E	R	Y	R	J	L	U	Y	A	M
B	Y	M	U	E	E	E	D	I	U	I	E	R	Y
U	S	R	M	Y	R	E	B	M	V	A	R	R	O
U	E	E	A	E	M	N	F	M	B	E	A	P	N
U	A	B	C	F	O	E	M	D	E	U	R	T	A
M	R	M	O	B	Y	R	N	U	R	V	R	N	U
Y	N	E	F	U	V	F	Y	B	U	Y	O	R	G
B	B	C	Y	A	M	H	E	E	A	T	N	N	U
M	E	E	M	T	C	F	N	N	R	R	N	S
A	C	D	J	R	H	T	U	B	E	N	U	J	T
Y	R	J	A	N	U	A	R	Y	U	J	M	R	R
F	U	M	U	N	E	U	E	E	C	F	Y	M	J

FEBRUARY
APRIL
JANUARY
OCTOBER
SEPTEMBER
DECEMBER
JULY
MAY
AUGUST
JUNE
MARCH
NOVEMBER

THE DAYS OF THE WEEK

Find the seven days of the week.

```
S  Z  B  X  I  A  L  X  I  H  A  U  R  U  X        FRIDAY
O  S  B  Z  B  Z  G  S  G  J  M  I  X  C  Z        MONDAY
M  S  P  W  H  Y  C  C  Y  J  Y  M  Q  E  H        SATURDAY
N  Z  Y  S  A  T  U  R  D  A  Y  C  A  F  S        SUNDAY
S  M  N  D  J  T  G  O  D  U  E  S  I  Q  F        THURSDAY
M  T  N  A  W  T  H  S  K  H  P  Y  Y  J  U        TUESDAY
N  O  Z  N  A  T  E  U  R  K  A  K  Z  G  H        WEDNESDAY
M  C  L  E  L  N  W  R  R  D  K  M  W  X  D
Z  V  U  U  D  J  O  F  N  S  O  I  C  V  N
P  I  Q  E  N  M  D  U  R  I  D  R  V  J  N
S  R  W  L  Q  I  S  X  B  I  F  A  Y  R  U
C  R  H  D  A  X  T  U  E  S  D  A  Y  Y  N
Y  W  P  T  Q  V  W  X  C  A  V  A  S  C  H
B  L  K  K  H  W  X  X  C  R  C  N  Y  X  O
W  I  W  X  O  R  G  O  L  K  T  E  K  O  D
```

...MORE, LESS + ADJECTIVE;
...THE MOST, THE LEAST + ADJECTIVE and MORE

Choose the correct answer to complete the sentence.

1) Some people think that London is among the _____ expensive cities in the world.
a) most
b) the most expensive
c) more expensive than
d) least expensive

2) This is _____ embarrassing option!
a) more than
b) less than
c) the least
d) the best

3) Do they really think that honey is _____ sugar?
a) healthy
b) healthiest
c) healthier than
d) the healthiest

4) What makes you say that spiders can be less _____ scorpions?
a) dangerous
b) poisonous than
c) lethal
d) the most dangerous

5) Winters in Sweden can be colder _____ winters in Portugal.
a) then
b) than
c) there
d) three

6) Their family is _____ important thing in the entire world.
a) more than
b) least
c) the most
d) most

7) Do you know that the cheetah can be _____ lions; with according to Wikipedia "the fastest reliably recorded speeds being 93 and 98 km/h"?
a) faster than
b) the fattest
c) the fastest
d) fat

8) The burger is _____ the whole meal.
a) less expensive
b) the most expensive
c) less expensive than
d) the least

10) The project team has shifted its attention to _____ options.
a) least
b) less than
c) the least damaging
d) the more damaged the

11) Waiting here seems _____ walking in the rain!
a) best
b) better than
c) the best
d) greatest

12) The students were truly thrilled. That was certainly _____ conference they had ever attended.
a) enriching
b) the most
c) the most fascinating
d) less

13) It's *not* going to work! That makes it the _____ business solution this century!
a) the best
b) worse
c) worst
d) the worst
e) worse than

WHO, WHY, WHERE, WHEN, WHAT, WHICH, WHOM, HOW

Choose the correct answer to complete the sentence.

1) That was the reason _____ the minister postponed his visit.
2) 2018 was _____ we bought the apartment.
3) Did he say _____ he was coming back?
4) The students chose the person _____ will be the class prefect.
5) The capital city is _____ the government main offices are.
6) Cars _____ are not parked properly will be clamped.
7) _____ is the man in the canteen?
8) Harry is the driver _____picked up the new employees from the airport.
9) _____ is the purpose of this gathering?
10) The student to _____ you gave the test just graduated.

11) _____ are the recruits supposed to complete the training without internet connection?
12) _____ are these boxes still on the floor?
13) Here is the book _____ cost the company £700!
14) The conference _____ changed the course of her career was delivered by Einstein himself.
15) The directors will vote on _____ supplier to select.
16) Captain Jones is the officer to _____ the cadets voiced their concerns.
17) They returned to the school _____ they completed their diploma.
18) _____ university do you wish to go to?
19) _____ tells you that he has changed?
20) If you don't tell them _____ took your bag; they can't do anything to get it back.
21) With _____ did Robert go to Prom?
22) Things got to the point _____ the partners had to get even bigger offices for the company.
23) _____ has the Dean's phone number?
24) This method is _____ got Prof. Brund his Nobel Prize.
25) _____ is why you must always use strong passwords for your account.
26) The river _____ crosses the country has greatly contributed to the development of agriculture.
27) Friday is _____ all spreadsheets are sent to headquarters.
28) The guide _____ showed you around is retiring next year.
29) The car _____ has wide wheels was designed in Norway.
30) They are waiting for you at the Café _____ you picked them up last Wednesday.
31) The graduate for _____ we bought the flowers is heading to Cambridge.
32) _____ in Wales is Donna buying the apartment; in _____ area?

33) Send us an email to let us know _____ to send the contractors.
34) The products _____ don't pass the quality standards must be reworked.
35) The trainees _____ complete the course will be awarded a scholarship.
36) The policeman told Arjun _____ he gave him a ticket.
37) Vicky doesn't want to hear _____ they have to say.
38) The books _____ explain grammar and vocabulary well are useful.
39) The guard explained _____ things happened.
40) We could not believe _____ we were hearing.
41) The street _____ we live is very quiet.
42) For _____ are the elected officials making those decisions?
43) _____ the time comes; we will find out the reason _____ the president lost the election.
44) _____ is Louise inviting to the wedding?
45) _____ could you expect him to believe such a story!?!
46) The students confirmed _____ the teacher told the Principal.
47) To _____ are you sending the flowers?
48) _____ it is time to board the planes, the hostesses will notify the passengers.
49) The town _____ their son lives is on the coast.
50) Don't reveal _____ you got the information from!

ABOUT, ACROSS, AFTER, AGAINST, AT, AS, BEFORE, BEHIND, BY, DURING, FOR, FROM, IN, INTO, OF, ON, THROUGH, TO, UP, WITH

Choose the correct answer to complete the sentence.

1) He works _____ the bank _____ an investment specialist.
2) The parcel has already been shipped _____ your home address.
3) Rita is coming _____ train.
4) Let's meet _____ the coffee shop _____ the street _____ 18:30.
5) The lecture was _____ clean energy.
6) Her family will always stand _____ her choices.
7) They will be hearing _____ her lawyers.
8) The new owner wants to have a word _____ all the employees.
9) Your refusal to apologise _____ the workers took the tension _____ a notch.
10) Refreshments will be served _____ the ceremony.
11) The car broke down _____ the motorway!
12) Mr. Adams put all his children _____ university.
13) They've now put this project _____ jeopardy.
14) The changes were announced _____ the meeting.
15) This project was like a race _____ time.
16) The construction work is now _____ hold.
17) The coach told the players to take their jerseys _____ them.
18) All _____ the staff members are still _____ lunch.
19) The committee has agreed to accept new members _____ the organisation.
20) _____ you board the plane; you will have to go _____ Security.
21) The garden is _____ the house.
22) The report is due _____ Wednesday.

23) The teacher printed enough booklets _____ the entire class.
24) Anita is _____ Spain.
25) They got _____ the bus.
26) In winter, they travel _____ Switzerland.
27) The commando was operating _____ enemy lines.
28) Mariam was talked _____ going _____ medical school _____ her brother.
29) Did you get the bottle _____ olive oil?
30) Meet them _____ Friday.
31) Did they crash _____ a tree?
32) _____ her presidency, she made long-lasting reforms.
33) It's a global corporation. They have offices literally _____ the world.
34)
- I am going _____ bed. Where are the children?
- They're already _____ bed.
35) After their second date, Aisha and Arun decided to take their relationship _____ the next level.
36) They usually warm _____ _____ their workout.
37) The government and the opposition must agree to talk _____ each other.
38) Remy joined the group _____ a choreographer.
39) The shop closed _____ noon.
40) Users must agree _____ these terms and conditions.
41) We can't possibly agree _____ these fabrications! We condemn them all, _____ the strongest possible terms.
42) Chloe responded _____ writing.
43) All interviews must be face _____ face.
44) The stunned audience just stared _____ the magician _____ silence.
45) The deliveryman parked _____ front _____ the house.
46) I apologise. That was utterly unwise _____ me and an opportunistic attempt _____ my part.

47) Yuki laid out the school uniforms _____ the bed _____ her children.

48) The matter will be discussed _____ great detail at the staff meeting.

49) The doctor is usually _____ his office _____ the morning.

50) The employees decided to take the matter _____ _____ the government.

NOUN + NOUN

Use a noun from each of the shaded boxes below to form a noun.

library	station	
action	call	
bank	park	
head	safety	
dining	certificate	
office	tie	
comfort	account	
plastic	rights	
diamond	camp	
train	room	
birth	teacher	
gender	agent	
boot	cake	
telephone	hours	
discount	office	
car	name	
silk	card	
cheese	ring	
exam	bag	
petrol	glove	
leather	results	
credit	book	
brand	station	
estate	movie	
voting	zone	
post	store	
road	equality	

SELECT THE CORRECT SENTENCE.

1 –
a) How do you like your meal, Sir?
b) Sir, do you like how your meal?
c) Your meal, Sir do you like how?
d) Do like you your Sir meal how?

2 –
a) Dare you don't like that speak me to!
b) To me like that dare speak don't you!
c) Don't you dare speak to me like that!
d) Speak to me dare like don't that you!

3 –
a) She her dogs missed must have lot a.
b) She a lot dogs have her must missed.
c) A lot she dogs her must missed have.
d) She must have missed her dogs a lot.

4 –
a) Outdoors together playing the children enjoy.
b) Playing outdoors the children enjoy together.
c) The children enjoy playing together outdoors.
d) Together outdoors children the enjoy playing.

5 –
a) None of the fans could see the singers.
b) See the singers none could of the fans.
c) The singers none of the could fans see.
d) Could none singers the fans of see the.

6 -
a) Seriously options were their weighing were.
b) They were seriously weighing their options.
c) Their were seriously they options weighing.
d) Options their they weighing were seriously.

7 –
a) Why hasn't anyone woken up the president?
b) Why anyone hasn't the president up woken?
c) Anyone the president woken hasn't up why?
d) The president why anyone woken up hasn't?

8 –
a) The villagers if they had made been aware more food much would have earlier brought.
b) Villagers the made been aware if they have earlier brought had more food much would.
c) The villagers would have brought much more food, if they had been made aware earlier.
d) Much more food, if the villagers would brought aware earlier made they made been had.

9 –
a) Dinner will be ready very soon.
b) Will be soon very ready dinner.
c) Ready very dinner soon be will.
d) Soon ready dinner will very be.

10 –
a) Eight project four-man compete teams the to took.
b) Four-man teams took eight project complete to the.
c) The project took eight four-man teams to complete.
d) To complete four-man took eight project the teams.

11-
a) There's no use insisting.
b) No insisting use there's.
c) Insisting use there's no.
d) No use insisting there's.

12-
a) We make sure all the urgent issues are dealt with swiftly.
b) Urgent swiftly make the sure issues dealt are with we all.
c) Dealt with sure make all are issues swiftly we the urgent.
d) Are dealt issues swiftly urgent sure the make with we all.

13 –
a) He who did give it to?
b) Who did he give it to?
c) Give it to who did he?
d) To it give he who did?

14 –
a) Outstanding all bonuses being are we paid as speak.
b) All outstanding bonuses are being paid as we speak.
c) Bonuses all speak paid outstanding are as we being.
d) All we speak outstanding being bonuses are paid as.

15 –
a) Agreed two managers have on these never anything!
b) These agreed two anything have managers never on!
c) On anything never agreed these have two managers!
d) These two managers have never agreed on anything!

16 –
a) What time were the children supposed to be back from the school trip?
b) From the school were the children what time supposed to be back trip?
c) Supposed what time children to be school trip back were the from the?
d) The children what time were from the school trip supposed to be back?

17 –
a) To the all been cancelled the flights region have.
b) The to region all the cancelled flights have been.
c) All been the the region have cancelled flights to.
d) All the flights to the region have been cancelled.

18 -
a) Want to I really do with that didn't have anything to!
b) I really to have anything didn't want with that to do!
c) Didn't want I really to have that anything to do with!
d) I really didn't want to have anything to do with that!

19 -
a) What is the alternative?
b) Is the what alternative?
c) What alternative is the?
d) The alternative what is?

20 -
a) We about nothing have to talk!
b) We have nothing to talk about!
c) Nothing we have to talk about!
d) Talk about we have nothing to!

REPORTED SPEECH

am/is/are able to,
can, will, may, might, must, would, could, should
was/were able to
had to

Turn the direct speech sentences into reported speech ones.

1 –
Roman: Sally, I can call you in one week.

John: What did Roman tell you, Sally?
Sally:

_____

_____

2 –
Roman: I am able to secure all the funds required.

John: What did Roman say?
Sally:

_____

_____

3 –
Roman: I will talk to new potential investors and partners.

John: What did Roman say?
Sally:

_____

_____

4 –

Roman: I may delay the board meeting.

John: What did Roman say?
Sally:

_____

_____

5 –

Roman: The builders should be notified as soon as possible.

John: What did Roman say?
Sally:

_____

_____

6 –

Roman: John, the driver is coming to pick you and Sally up at the airport.

Sally: John, what did Roman tell you?
John:

_____

_____

7 –

Roman: John, you don't need to bring your own Laptop.

Sally: What did Roman tell you?
John:

_____

_____

8 –

Roman: Sally, you and John might want to bring all you will need for the tennis exhibition.

John: What did Roman tell you?
Sally:

_____

_____

9 –

Roman: We could launch the new product a lot earlier.

Sally: What did Roman say?
John:

_____

_____

10 –

Roman: We must make this event a resounding success!

Sally: What did Roman say?
John:

_____

_____

PHRASAL VERBS

Nouns and pronouns
Select all the sentences that mean the same as the sentence in **bold.**

1 -
a) **The aides will now work out the details of the contract.**
b) The aides will now work it out.
c) The aides will now work them out.
d) The aides will now work them out it.
e) The aides will now work it out the details of the contract.

2 –
a) Germany turned it down.
b) **Germany turned down France's help.**
a) Germany turned them down.
a) Germany turned it them down France's help.

3 –
a) We are looking it up in the dictionary.
b) We are looking them up words in the dictionary.
c) **We are looking up words in the dictionary.**
d) We are looking up words in the dictionary it them.

4 –
a) They threw ours away.
b) **They threw away our belongings.**
c) They threw it away.
d) They threw them away.
e) They threw our away.

5 –
a) The soldiers took them over.
b) They took over the entire country.
c) They took it over.
d) The soldiers took it over the entire country.
e) They took it them over the entire country.
f) **The soldiers took over the entire country.**

6 –
a) **The builders are tearing down the old library.**
b) They builders are tearing it down the old library.
c) They are tearing them down.
d) The builders are tearing it down the old library.
e) There builders are tearing down the old library.

7 –
a) **The company doesn't want to pay off its debt!**
b) The company doesn't want to pay them off!
c) The company doesn't want to pay it off!
d) It doesn't want to pay off its debt!
e) It doesn't want to pay it off!

8 –
a) **The authorities closed down all the illegal discotheques.**
b) The authorities closed them down.
c) They closed them all down.
d) They closed them illegal discotheques down.
e) The authorities closed it down.

9 –
a) We are not calling it off!
b) **We are not calling off the search!**
c) We are not calling them off!
d) We aren't calling off the search!
e) We aren't calling it off!
f) We are not calling it them off!

10 –
a) She is backing up her arguments with substantial evidence.
b) She's backing them up with substantial evidence.
c) The lawyer is backing it up her arguments with substantial evidence.
d) **The lawyer is backing up her arguments with substantial evidence.**
e) She is backing it up with substantial evidence.

11 -
a) **Chelsea turned off the TV.**
b) She turned it off.
c) Chelsea turned off it.
d) She turned them off.
e) Chelsea turned it off the TV.

12 -
a) They put on his shoes.
b) She put on his shoes.
c) He put it on.
d) He put on his shoes.
e) He put them on.
f) **Freddy put on his shoes.**

13 -
a) The neighbours have given it up smoking.
b) The neighbours have given it up.
c) **The neighbours have given up smoking.**
d) They have given up smoking.
e) They've given it up.
f) They have given them up.

14 -
a) **The DJ turns the volume up.**
b) The DJ turns up the volume.
c) He turns it up.
d) He turns them up.
e) The DJ turns the volume up it.
f) The DJ turned it up.

15 -
a) Don't bring it up those matters, please.
b) Do not bring them up, please.
c) Don't bring them up, please.
d) Please, do not bring up those matters.
e) **Don't bring up those matters, please.**
f) Don't bring up them those matters, please.

16 –
a) They are filling out the application forms.
b) John and Sara are filling them out.
c) They are filling out them.
d) **John and Sara are filling out the application forms.**
e) John and Sara are filling it out.
f) John and Sara are filling them it out.

HOW... + ADJECTIVES questions and answers
WHAT IS THE... + NOUNS questions and answers

Choose the correct word to complete the sentence.

cold, tall, far, hot, deep, heavy, high, wide, long, old width, temperature, depth, age, height, distance, length, weight

1-
- How _____ is the Universal Declaration of Human Rights?
- It's 74 years old.

2 -
- How _____ was the old truck?
- It was about 4000 kilograms.

3 –
- How hot should the oven be for this cake?
- The _____ should be 220 degrees Celsius.

4 –
- How old is your teacher?
- Mr. Abdullah is 45 years of _____.

- He is very _____.
- His actual _____ is 2,01 metres.

5 –
- Be careful lifting that box. It is very heavy.
- You are right. It says: "_____: 75kg" on this label.

6 –
- What's the _____ of the table?
- It is 50 centimetres wide.

7 -
-   What's the length of the conference?
-   It's only one hour _____.

8 –
-   How _____ is the office from here?
-   The office is three kilometres away.

9 –
-   How _____ is the lake?
-   Its width is 300 metres.

-   Do you know its _____?
-   It's only 25 metres deep.

10 –
-   How long is the Nile River (in Africa)?
-   Its _____ is 6650 kilometres.

11 –
-   How _____ the Sahara Desert?
-   Wikipedia says "The average annual temperature is 30°C, whilst the hottest temperature ever recorded was 58°C".

12 –
-   What is the _____ between London and Paris.
-   It's 344 kilometres.

13 –
-   How _____ is the well?
-   It's 3 metres deep.

14 –
-   Burj Khalifa is the tallest/highest building in the world.
-   How _____ is it?
-   It's 829,8 metres (_____).

15 –
- How _____ is ice cream?
- It's -18 degrees Celsius or colder.

16 –
- How _____ is the Eiffel Tower, Paris?
- It's 330 metres _____.

BONUS QUESTIONS
- Usain Bolt is deemed the fastest man on earth!
- How _____ is he?

- Warren Buffet and Jeff Bezos are some of the richest men alive!
- How _____ are they?

- How _____ am I?
- You should have been here 20 minutes ago!

- Oh, no! The engine is leaking and the mechanic can't fix it!
- How _____ is it?

- We will buy the sofa at the end of the month. Let's save a bit more.
- How _____ is it?

Put the sentence's number
opposite the CORRECT CORRESPONDING TENSE.
Example: **Present** perfect continuous - 16
There can be more than one sentence per tense.

1)	I am studying for my exams.
2)	They were going on holiday.
3)	Anita will have completed her course.
4)	Dr. Choudhuri is in her office.
5)	The children haven't seen their pets for days!
6)	The neighbours had seen all the events.
7)	Nourah has not been in Europe for a long time.
8)	The entire team will be traveling to Peru.
9)	Why will Raoul move in with his parents?
10)	The new administration will have been running the country for a month.
11)	Sameh had been working for IBM.
12)	The guards haven't heard anything.
13)	The secretary will call you.
14)	The meeting started early.
15)	Lisa wasn't in the kitchen.
16)	**It has been raining for days.**

PAST	Perfect continuous	
	Perfect	
	Continuous	
	Simple	
PRESENT	Perfect continuous	**16**
	Perfect	
	Continuous	
	Simple	
FUTURE	Perfect continuous	
	Perfect	
	Continuous	
	Simple	

SPORTS and THEIR AREAS

Write the correct corresponding area (below) opposite the right sport(s).

rink, alley, track, range, field, mat or tatami, court, ring, course, table, and pool.

Example:
- golf course
- **swimming pool**

Sports	Areas
- boxing - wrestling	
- tennis - squash - handball - netball - volleyball - basketball - kabaddi - badminton	
- **golf**	course
- soccer - American football - baseball - polo - cricket	
- athletics - car racing - horse racing	
- bowling	
- ice skating - hockey - figure skating	
- **swimming**	pool
- pool - table tennis	

- archery - shooting	
- judo - karate - taekwondo	

Ingram Content Group UK Ltd.
Milton Keynes UK
UKHW050507280323
419244UK00006B/128